Perils, Pitfalls and Reflexivity in
Qualitative Research
in Education

Perils, Pitfalls and Reflexivity in Qualitative Research in Education

Editors
Fauzia Shamim
Rashida Qureshi

OXFORD
UNIVERSITY PRESS

OXFORD
UNIVERSITY PRESS

Great Clarendon Street, Oxford OX2 6DP

Oxford University Press is a department of the University of Oxford.
It furthers the University's objective of excellence in research, scholarship,
and education by publishing worldwide in

Oxford New York

Auckland Cape Town Dar es Salaam Hong Kong Karachi
Kuala Lumpur Madrid Melbourne Mexico City Nairobi
New Delhi Shanghai Taipei Toronto

With offices in

Argentina Austria Brazil Chile Czech Republic France Greece
Guatemala Hungary Italy Japan Poland Portugal Singapore
South Korea Switzerland Turkey Ukraine Vietnam

Oxford is a registered trademark of Oxford University Press
in the UK and in certain other countries

ISBN 978-0-19-547948-5

Typeset in Adobe Caslon Pro
Printed in Pakistan by
Pixel Graphix, Karachi.
Published by
Ameena Saiyid, Oxford University Press
No. 38, Sector 15, Korangi Industrial Area, P.O. Box 8214,
Karachi-74900, Pakistan.

Contents

	page
Acknowledgments	vii
Note from the Editors	viii
Preface	x

Section I:
Research North and South
Introduction
Fauzia Shamim and Rashida Qureshi 2

1. Submission, emergence, and personal knowledge: New takes and principles for validity in decentred qualitative research 10
Adrian Holliday

Section II:
Qualitative Research in the South: Focus on Ethics

2. Ethical dilemmas in research with young children: A field experience from Pakistan 32
Almina Pardhan

3. Obligations, roles, and rights: Research ethics revisited 59
Saiqa Imtiaz Asif

4. Ethical standards and ethical environment: Tensions and a way forward 78
Rashida Qureshi

Section III:
Qualitative Research in the South: Focus on Methodology

5. Using a feminist standpoint for
    researching women's lives in the
    rural mountainous areas of Pakistan   101
    Dilshad Ashraf

6. The complexity of researching the
    lives of women school leaders in Kenya   127
    Jane F.A. Rarieya

7. Experience and identity: The ethnographer
    as a practising artist   148
    Mehri Honarbin-Holliday

8. Performing methodological activities in
    post-colonial ethnographic encounters:
    Examples from Oaxaca, Mexico   170
    Ángeles Clemente and Michael Higgins

Appendix: The two versions of a poem   191

Editors   192

Contributors   193

Acknowledgments

We would like to acknowledge the encouragement and patronage of Professor Dr Muhammad Shamsuddin, former Dean, Faculty of Arts, University of Karachi, Pakistan, in holding the first multidisciplinary international conference on 'Qualitative research in developing countries: possibilities and challenges' at the University of Karachi in November 2006, which became the impetus for this collection of papers. We would also like to thank all the contributors for their patience and hard work in producing multiple drafts of their chapters. Our thanks to Uzma Abdul Rashid, co-operative teacher, Department of English, University of Karachi, for her editorial help.

Note from the Editors

This book has grown out of a need that we felt while teaching qualitative research methods courses to graduate students at the Aga Khan University–Institute of Educational Development in Karachi, Pakistan[1]. We found that while a range of methods texts were available for beginning researchers that introduce the students to the 'what' and 'how' of various approaches within the qualitative paradigm (e.g. Bogdan and Biklen, 2007; Creswell, 2003; Glesne, 1999; Denzin and Lincoln, 2005; Maxwell, 2005; Merriam, 1998) and to writing qualitative research (e.g. Holliday, 2007), the voices of indigenous researchers undertaking qualitative research within novel research environments such as that of our students, were conspicuous by their absence. The stories of 'local' researchers, even if available, are few and far between, possibly due to publishing constraints in these contexts (Salager-Meyer, 2008). Hence there is little opportunity for novice researchers to prepare for the kinds of methodological and ethical challenges they might face in the field in conducting research in international contexts, particularly in countries in the South. Consequently, the need for potential researchers in these contexts to 'hear' and learn from field stories, particularly the ways in which researchers have addressed methodological and ethical dilemmas faced in the specific social-cultural context of their 'local' research environments cannot be over emphasized.

Conferences and seminars provide a platform for novice researchers to learn with and from each other and from more experienced researchers through sharing their research experiences and the issues faced during data collection and analysis. One such opportunity was provided by the University of Karachi by organizing an international conference in November 2006 on 'Qualitative research in developing countries:

possibilities and challenges'.[2] Majority of the chapters in this book have been developed from papers presented at this conference. However, chapters Four, Seven and Eight were commissioned especially for this book.

How to use this book

The book can be used to supplement methods books in qualitative undergraduate and graduate level courses offered both in developing countries in the South as well as the more developed countries in the North. The field stories presented by indigenous researchers can be read individually or discussed in research seminars. The aim is to make current and prospective researchers aware of the perils and pitfalls in undertaking qualitative research in countries in the South, and the role of reflexivity in ensuring the validity of their data and findings in these and similar contexts elsewhere.

Notes

1. Students at the Aga Khan University come from Pakistan and other developing countries in South and Central Asia, East Africa, and Syria.
2. One of the editors, who currently works at the University of Karachi, initiated this idea and was the convener of the conference.

References

Bogdan, R.C., and Biklen, S.K., *Qualitative Research for Education*, 2e (Boston, USA: Allyn & Bacon, 2007).

Creswell, J.W., *Research Design: Qualitative, Quantitative and Mixed Approaches*, 2e (Thousand Oaks, CA: Sage Publications Inc., 2003).

Denzin, N.K., and Lincoln, Y.S. (eds.), *The Sage Handbook of Qualitative Research*, 3e (Thousand Oaks, CA: Sage Publications Ltd., 2005).

Glesne, C., *Becoming Qualitative Researchers* (USA: Longman, 1999).

Holliday, A.R., *Doing and Writing Qualitative Research*, 2e (London: Sage, 2007).

Maxwell, J.A., *Qualitative Research Design*, 2e (California: Sage, 2005).

Merriam, S.B., *Qualitative Research and Case Study Applications in Education* (San Francisco: Jossey-Bass, 1998).

Salager-Meyer, F., 'Scientific Publishing in Developing Countries: Challenges for the Future', *Journal of English for Academic Purposes*, 7 (2008), 121–132.

Preface

As the editors indicate, this volume will help firstly fill a gap for many working in 'the South' regarding how they might approach qualitative research. Whilst methods books claim to offer general accounts of such an approach, in practice what is to be found in most such volumes is based on assumptions and data from research in the North. The authors of the present volume have recognized that the 'voices of indigenous researchers undertaking qualitative research within research environments' in the South, such as those of their own students, are absent from such accounts. How then to help these students and their colleagues to engage in qualitative research that is relevant to their own environments? The present book addresses this question through both methodological reflexivity regarding such work (as in the introduction by the editors and the opening chapter by Professor Adrian Holliday), and through detailed case studies by researchers working in the South. A strength of this volume is the variety and detail of such accounts, ranging from work in Pakistan where the editors themselves are situated, to accounts from Kenya, Iran and Mexico. In addition, a number of the chapters address ethical issues in qualitative research and consider what reflexivity, which has become a key concept in qualitative research in the North, might mean in environments in the South. Several chapters also bring the general insights to bear on work within the universities themselves, where the authors work and struggle to help their students—and colleagues. As the editors state in the Introduction, it is hoped thereby to stimulate such researchers 'develop their own indigenous solutions to the challenges faced during their field work'.

This book is not solely addressed to those working in the South. It will also be vital reading for those working in the North. At the first level, it will open the eyes of many experienced as well as beginning researchers in the North to the limits of the methodological underpinnings and ethical claims regarding their own research traditions. This has implications both for those continuing to research in the North, as it exposes to critical gaze the assumptions, methodological and ethical that they might otherwise take for granted. And secondly, for the many researchers who currently seek to bridge the 'North/South' divide it opens up new vistas for how they might move across, not only collecting data in southern environments, but bringing southern perspectives to bear on their own research in the North and developing new hybrid traditions to keep pace with the new 'hybridity' at the level of the data itself. It is being increasingly recognized that people now move across the old boundaries—migrants, refugees, bankers and academics to name just a few categories in what a recent anthropological book termed the 'New Cosmopolitanism' (cf Werbner, 2008). Authors such as Robinson-Pant (2005), for instance, have focused on the movement of international students to universities in the North and their subsequent return to academic environments in the South, again combining insights and understandings from both in ways that are central to the editors' focus in the present volume.

In the light of these new experiences and approaches, the old traditions of inquiry and the old methods handbooks are struggling to keep pace with both the data and the research traditions for investigating it. The present book, then, is at an early stage of this growing movement and will provide those alert to the shifts with a rich and soundly argued set of data and methods for addressing them. As the editors suggest in the Introduction, 'the book seeks to present the voices of researchers from the South' and it clearly has a major contribution in making these more visible. They hope, for instance, that their 'reflexive accounts of conducting research in varied socio-cultural settings will help potential educational researchers in preparation for embarking on their studies in similar contexts'. But a key contribution will also be for those embarking on studies in the

North too, as they are forced to come to terms with the new hybrid character of social data. It is this hybridity, in both content and research, that provides the rich environment for such a timely new volume.

Professor Brian Street
King's College, London.

References

Robinson-Pant, A., *Cross-cultural Perspectives on Educational Research* (Buckingham: Open University Press, 2005).

Werbner, P. (ed.), *Anthropology and the New Cosmopolitanism* (Oxford: Berg/ASA Monographs, 2008).

Section I

Research North and South

Introduction

FAUZIA SHAMIM AND RASHIDA QURESHI

The book seeks to present the voices of researchers from the South, particularly their reflexive accounts of conducting research in varied socio-cultural settings in developing countries. The aim is to help potential educational researchers in preparation for embarking on their studies in similar contexts. Additional aims for presenting this collection of papers are: making a humble contribution to the current debate on the 'geo-politics of knowledge production', and encouraging the participation of researchers in the South in developing contextually appropriate methodologies and ethical practices for emergence of local knowledge, in ways that may not be possible through the use of methodologies developed solely in the North.

The contributions in the book are based on research conducted in various settings in countries in the South. The researchers are mainly insiders-outsiders, who keep shifting positions on the insider-outsider continuum as they struggle to make sense of their training in academic institutions in the North and their understandings of the local culture and its demands on the researcher as well as methodological and ethical decision making during field work. In all the accounts, these indigenous researchers show a great deal of sensitivity to the methodological and ethical dilemmas posed by their unique position in the research setting (often considered more equal than others due to their education level, affiliation with a university in the North etc.); more important, they show how they can be proactive and address these dilemmas through taking a 'reflexive turn' (Foley, 2002). Incorporating reflexive practices into their research work seems to empower them to present confidently their decisions in the field, which are often incongruent with the rules written in methods textbooks or those prescribed by Ethics Review Committees of universities in the North. Reflexivity thus helps them in acknowledging the subjectivities inherent in qualitative research in education while allowing them to address the methodological and ethical dilemmas faced in the field.

The book is divided into three sections: Section I comprises the introduction and chapter one. Section II has three chapters focusing mainly on ethical issues. Section III presents, in four chapters, examples of how researchers in the South, in identifying and addressing methodological issues in the field, are beginning to participate not only in 'the production of new knowledge but in *how* that knowledge is to be attained or collected, that is, *methodology*' (Clemente and Higgins, chapter 8).

The aim of Section I is to highlight issues in qualitative research in relation to North/South research, and how reflexivity is at the core of doing valid research particularly in the largely unexplored research environments in the South. In chapter One, **Holliday** discusses how in qualitative research the rules for validity are realized very differently to the way they are realized in quantitative research. The underlying aim is the same—to make the research disciplined and hence scientific. Qualitative research is also disciplined and scientific, but with the specific purpose of confronting directly the intensely subjective nature of social research. Whereas quantitative research tries to control variables, qualitative research seeks the proliferation and richness of variables. Whereas quantitative research tries to reduce the impact of the researcher, qualitative research acknowledges and capitalizes on the impact of the researcher. Indeed, a major aim of qualitative research is 'to reveal hidden and counter cultures— to demonstrate that things are different to what we thought they were' (p. 12). Holliday explores the validity of qualitative research by looking at three principles, i.e., submission, emergence and personal knowledge, and how they operate in examples of data: 'They require that researchers must *submit* themselves to what they see and hear by consciously and strategically being aware of and managing their own prejudices about how things are.

Submission allows realities which are beyond the initial vision of the re-searcher to *emerge*; an essential measure of valid qualitative research is that something has been done to enable the unexpected. Researchers are able to assess the validity of their findings by setting them against their own unprejudiced personal *knowledge* of the broad nature of social life' (p. 12).

Section II has three chapters. The focus is mainly on identifying ethical issues in relation to different socio-cultural 'norms' of behavior and ways of addressing the potential conflict created due to a dissonance between these 'local' norms (and participant expectations)and international guidelines. It is interesting to note that despite the huge expansion in the use of qualitative methods in research, there is relatively little discussion on the ethical and methodological issues in relation to researching with children. The limited information available on research methods with young children is rooted primarily in research with young children in Western contexts. As such, **Pardhan** (chapter Two) embarked on her study with few guideposts on research in non-western contexts and had to draw upon those that were primarily from a Western perspective and found herself grappling with many complex practical and ethical issues in her research with children in a developing context. Pardhan discusses, the tensions and ethical dilemmas she encountered conducting research with children in relation to: notions of children and childhood in the Pakistani context and her own beliefs about children; negotiating her presence and building a relationship of trust with the children (both the research participants and non-research participants); issues of consent and assent; and researching the experiences of child research participants.

Educational research in Pakistan, like other disciplines, is expected to follow ethical guidelines mainly derived from the professional codes of conduct provided by the American Educational Research Association (AERA) and/or by the British Educational Research Association (BERA). However, the context of research is governed by the code(s) of conduct embedded in local culture and practices. Thus social scientists in

Pakistan including educational researchers, are caught in a position where they have to adapt the codes and practices prescribed by Associations working in vastly different contexts in the North. In their struggle to keep the 'conduct' and 'context' of research together, 'local' researchers in the South are faced with important ethical dilemmas which raise both general and practical questions for them as researchers as well as for the discipline as a whole. The decision to conduct research may present a conflict between different sets of values: the commitment of the researcher to expanding knowledge, and the cost of research to the participants. The research project or practices may also conflict with moral, cultural and religious principles. It is often not possible to resolve such conflicts by a set of prescriptions that will cover all cases. As mentioned before, while several professional organizations and universities provide a set of 'recipes' for resolving ethical choices or dilemmas, it is not often recognized that the researchers need to make such choices on the basis of principles, values and interests of those involved in the local setting. **Asif**, during the course of her doctoral research, discovered that the reality of the writers of the guide books about research practices was different from the reality she encountered in the field in Pakistan. Asif discusses, in chapter Three, her ethical dilemma when she found that issues related to Informed Consent and signing of Consent Form with reference to her research participants did not fit in with the neatly laid down ethical code for research prescribed by a British university where she was enrolled as a doctoral student. Therefore, in view of her experiences in the field, Asif emphasizes the critical importance of the need for establishing codes of ethics for local researchers working in different disciplines. This issue, of course, also arises for those in the North and it is perhaps through the increased emphasis on comparison with the South, of the kind evident in the present volume, that such researchers can come to reflect more critically on their own taken for granted assumptions.

Similarly, **Qureshi** describes, in chapter Four, ethical dilemmas faced in the course of her own research and that of her graduate students in diverse educational settings. In the light of these experiences, she argues for a position of 'limited cultural pluralism' to deal with the ethical issues faced by many 'local' researchers due to a tension between internationally developed and agreed upon 'ethical standards' and indigenous 'ethical environments'. Qureshi concludes her chapter by exemplifying how this approach as currently used at the Aga Khan University in Karachi, Pakistan, seeks to foster researcher integrity without compromising international ethical standards or the specific socio-cultural requirements of different research settings.

Section III comprises four chapters (5–8) focusing on methodological issues and innovative ways in which the researchers tried to address them in different research settings in Pakistan, Kenya, Iran and Mexico. **Ashraf**, in chapter Five, examines methodological and ethical issues in researching lives of five women teachers in the Northern Areas of Pakistan. Taking a feminist perspective, she used the life history approach and observation to study the lives of these women within the broader cultural, societal, and professional context of the region. Playing the roles of outsider-insider and insider-outsider, Ashraf was able to build her research around the principles of visibility of women's voices, reciprocity and elimination of power relationship between herself, the researcher, and her research participants. Her identity as a local female contributed to women's immediate approval of her presence in their lives as they considered her their sister. Resulting from this trust was sharing of confidential information (sometimes about intimate relationships) with the researcher, that, in accordance to local culture, women would not disclose generally. This nature of relationships posed methodological and ethical dilemmas as the researcher was often not sure whether she should act as a researcher or react to the situation as a 'sister' or a local woman. Taking a reflexive stance, Ashraf analyzes these methodological and ethical tensions faced while researching women's lives in the mountain communities. Some suggestions for the viability of researching women's experiences with feminist perspective in contexts similar to that of the study are offered in conclusion.

Literature is replete with studies and books that seek to provide clarity on the nature, purposes and processes of conducting qualitative research. Hence, when most researchers embark on qualitative research they go to the field armed with a well-rehearsed 'How to do' list. However, little is ever discussed about the complexities of conducting qualitative educational research in contexts where there is little or no such research activity. Although the discipline of anthropology has traditionally claimed special expertise in this area and is currently producing books that complement the present volume (e.g. Werbner, 2008), it is becoming increasingly apparent that the antimony presented by the particularity and universality of qualitative research needs greater emphasis on work in an international context that bridges the traditional North/South divide. **Rareiya,** in chapter Six, presents her experiences as a researcher in conducting a qualitative study on the lives of women school leaders in Kenya. She highlights the multiple complexities that she faced in conducting such a qualitative study in the setting of a developing country like Kenya. These broadly range from issues related to entering the field and gathering data to the appropriateness of the research topic itself. Also, ethical issues that arose during the study due to the specific study context (a developing country) and their impact on the 'trustworthiness' of the research process are discussed. The chapter demonstrates that qualitative research is as much specific as it is universal, thereby highlighting the central role of reflexivity in the research process in qualitative studies.

In chapter Seven, **Honarbin-Holliday** reports on how she used concepts from multidisciplinary theoretical sources as 'the researcher's tools' for a better understanding of the field, the participants, 'ideological positioning', and to create a space to juxtapose written and visual texts in order to facilitate wider epistemologies and hermeneutics. She also argues for ethnographic texts traditionally represented in words to include "visual, oral, and behavioural as in 'performance' art".

Chapter Eight, the final chapter, presents the experiences of two researchers, **Clemente and Higgins**, in what they describe as the post-colonial context in Oaxaca, Mexico. More specifically, the two researchers illustrate 'the dynamics of coevalness' in a range of ethnographic encounters. The context for their various methodological performances include: an overall investigation into the composition and performance in English of the students at the language center at the state university in Oaxaca; an emerging encounter on cultural literacy practices among inmates at the state prison in Oaxaca; and an account of poor young urban students learning English in a local primary school in the city of Oaxaca. These methodological performances, enacted in shared time and spaces with the research participants, allow for emergence of local knowledge that, it is claimed, would not have been possible through the use of more traditional ethnographic methods. The authors illustrate, significantly, how ethnographic methods can be 'composed or performed in order to decolonize the control [of the North] over knowledge production'.

The reflexivity evident in all the accounts, we hope, would stimulate beginning researchers develop their own indigenous solutions to the challenges faced during their field work, and in the writing and dissemination of their work both for the local and a more international audience. More important, reading and reflecting on these accounts would prepare them to deal with these and similar issues reflexively and, therefore, responsibly during the course of their own research. We trust that, in turn, these researchers will be able to take these discourses forward through disseminating their stories to the wider academic community in future publications.

References

Folley, D.E., 'Critical Ethnography: the Reflexive Turn', *Qualitative Studies in Education* 13(5) (2002), 469–490.

Werbner, P. (ed.), *Anthropology and the New Cosmopolitanism* (Oxford: Berg/ ASA Monographs, 2008).

1

Submission, emergence, and personal knowledge

New takes and principles for validity in decentred qualitative research

ADRIAN HOLLIDAY

One of the biggest tasks in qualitative research is working out how to proceed within a set of practices which are now more or less established as immensely subjective. The reflexivity associated with this is deep, requiring researchers to engage both with their own subjectivity as well as the subjective complexity of social life. This realization, and the acceptance of the inevitable nature of subjectivity, has grown out of a paradigm shift between a more established postpositivist position to a postmodern position. The *postpositivist* position retains aspects of a positivist paradigm. It holds on to the idea that objective truths can be described by means of systematic scanning of the territory through sampling and triangulation, or by extended surveillance in naturalistic ethnography, and that the researcher can be an impartial, distanced, unobtrusive, 'fly-on-the-wall' figure. This characterization of postpositivism is set out by its critics (e.g. Gubrium and Holstein, 1997: 19–33; Guba and Lincoln, 2005; Hammersley and Atkinson, 1995: 1; Holliday, 2007: 16). The 'alternative' *postmodern* paradigm is associated with critical theory, feminism, constructivism, and participatory and cooperative approaches (Lincoln and Guba, 2000). It rejects the 'naïve' postpositivist view of reality, and asserts that social truths and research methodologies are mediated by ideological, social and political forces; that objectivity cannot be avoided; and that the researcher is interactively, reflexively implicated within the research setting (e.g. Gubrium and Holstein, 1997: 9; Hammersley and Atkinson, 1995: 16; Faubion, 2001). This paradigm shift within ethnography and social anthropology has also been associated with the publication of Clifford and Marcus's (1986) *Writing Culture* (Spencer, 2001; MacDonald, 2001), which asserts 'the constructed, artificial nature of cultural accounts' (Clifford, 1986: 2).

In this chapter I will present three principles—of submission, emergence, and personal knowledge—as a means of establishing rigour and disciplined within a postmodern research methodology, to counter the accusation of being 'unsystematic'. I will also demonstrate, with reference to a series of research projects, how both a postmodern approach and an application of these principles has particular value in decentred research, where it is of paramount importance to allow what Bhabha (1994) refers to as 'vernacular' cultural realities to emerge in their own terms. Decentred research is by no means necessarily the projection of a Periphery voice against a Centre construction of how things are. I see it as the ultimate responsibility of critical qualitative research, in any circumstance, to make visible the unexpected for the purpose of revealing deeper complexities that counter established discourses.

Much of the material I cite, from my own research and that of colleagues and students, has been referred to elsewhere (e.g. Holliday, 2007). However, the act of putting it together, in new juxtapositions, within the format of this chapter, has led me to new insights about the relationships between the researcher's different 'takes' on the same research field phenomena—and how the three principles of submission, emergence, and personal knowledge provide a measure for valuing take 2 over take 1 in each case.

An alternative view of validity

The three principles are derived from observation of actual research practice, as a product of making sense of how researchers are able to do what they do. They require that researchers must *submit* themselves to what they see and hear, by consciously and strategically being aware of and managing their own prejudices about how things are. Submission allows realities which are beyond the initial vision of the researcher to *emerge*; an essential measure of valid qualitative research is that something has been done to enable the unexpected. Researchers are able to assess the validity of their findings by setting them against their own unprejudiced *personal knowledge* of the broad nature of social life.

The implication here is that the rules for validity are realized very differently to the way they would be in a postpositivist paradigm. They share a common underlying aim—to make the research disciplined and hence scientific, but the purpose with postmodern qualitative research is different. Whereas in postpositivist research the aim is to control variables in an attempt to reduce the impact of the researcher, in postmodern qualitative research the aim is to seek the proliferation and richness of variables, to acknowledge and capitalize on the impact of the researcher, and to have no fear of travelling to the hidden depths and mysterious complexities of reality. This is particularly relevant where the aim is to reveal hidden and counter cultures and to demonstrate that things are different to what we thought they were. I use the term 'scientific' here broadly. Qualitative research *is* scientific, but in a different way, in that meaning is pursued in a *disciplined* manner which is *accountable*—an accountability through showing the workings (Holliday, 2007). Clifford Geertz, in *The Interpretation of Culture*, states that 'what makes a study convincing...is whether it sorts winks from twitches and real winks from mimicked ones' (1993: 16). He demonstrates this in his (1993: 6) account of Ryle's analysis of two boys standing in a square, both moving the lid on one eye rapidly. To find out whether each one is winking or twitching it is necessary to go outside the core of the instance and investigate what is going on amongst a group of boys standing some distance away. It then emerges that one boy is twitching and that the other is winking in parody of the other one to entertain the wider group. There is thus a persistent pursuance of evidence as the researcher strives to get to the bottom of things.

Examples from the field

While it is important to acknowledge that qualitative research is an interdisciplinary activity, my examples are mainly educational because this is my experience. What I say about them is however informed by a wider range of secondary experience from health, sport science, business, women's studies, and so on (Holliday, 2007).

Example 1: Egyptian girls' school

My first example is from Herrera's (1992) use of thick description in her study of a girls' secondary school in Cairo. One of the themes which she selects as significant from her six-month ethnographic immersion in the culture of the school is the headmistress—her 'life, attitudes, struggles, relationships, confrontations, aspirations'. She constructs her interpretation of this by juxtaposing a broad range of instances represented by a series of data types: a description of her dealing with a pupil, a description of what happens when she enters a class, a description of her role in the school, a description of her office and its artefacts, her account of her mission in the school, a student's account of her effect on timekeeping, and a clause in the role of the headmistress in a ministry document. This leads to an effective thick description (Holliday, 2007: 74).

However, on what basis can it be established that what Herrera claims is not just a product of her own imagination, which has led her to select what suits her, and to read into it what she wishes in her analysis? I will now leave this example pending, and use the following examples to help me answer this question. I will then return to Herrera's study at the end of the chapter to reassess it in the light of what I have learnt.

Example 2: Chinese high school students

Duan (2007), in his study of the impact of the Chinese national university entrance exam on final year high school students, had several choices about how to proceed in data collection and analysis. Figure 1 lists two of these choices. I refer to the one on the left as *standard* because it is a common formulation I have seen in a large number of research papers and student dissertations. It is however very unsatisfactory because it is too researcher-led and leaves no room for the unexpected. The questions are generated by the researcher's first ideas about what to look for, the investigation is generated directly by the questions, and the outcome is a set of answers generated directly by both of these. Duan chose the second option, which I feel is more appropriate because it represents a creative *exploration*, not only of the field of study, but also of the way in which the methodology might best develop.

Figure 1: Methodological choices

Standard	Exploratory
[1] Observe classes, interviewing students and teachers, within a school case study	[a] Visit an unfamiliar UK school to practice observation skills, and acquire the discipline of making the familiar strange
[2] Devise interview questions … and observation checklists	[b] Notice the complexity of the school, its hidden discourses, and 'strange' student behaviour
	[c] Carry out informal conversations with recent Chinese school leavers
[3] Ask the questions. Tick the boxes	[d] Discover the emergent, creative, exploratory nature of conversations
[4] Record the answers	[e] Learn to submit himself to what he found along the way until the unexpected begins to emerge

His visit to the UK primary school (Figure 1 [a]) was a training task which I set him for the purpose of sharpening his eye for seeing the unexpected. It was the school which his daughter was attending during his study period in the UK, which gave him an introduction to the setting. He observed a number of classes; and because they were unfamiliar, he noticed the deeper workings of the politics and discourses of the classroom. This would enable him, later, to see some of the realities of the more familiar school in China that he had not hitherto noticed. The gaze of 'the stranger' is an essential dimension of good research (Schutz, 1964). His initial interactions with subjects thus also became more cautious and exploratory as he continued to find and develop his interview approach. Referring to 'conversations' instead of 'interviews' in itself comprised a problematizing of the norm—a problematizing of the researcher thinking-as-usual, which must be interrogated if the thinking-as-usual of the field and the subjects is to be interrogated.

Discovering the unexpected

There are important ethnographic rules here, which connect with the disciplines of submission and emergence—that one cannot proceed as planned until one works out how to present oneself as a researcher, and that one cannot decide what to do next until one has entered the field and begun to come to terms with it. Researchers must *submit* themselves to the nature of the place and then discover more than they imagined about their subjects. An example of this is where Herrera (op cit) discovered after some time in the field that teachers in the school would not allow her into their classes until they established that she was not just an American student, but also a mother and a wife. Shamim (1996) similarly found that what was most meaningful to teachers in her study of a secondary school in Pakistan was that she was the friend of a friend of one of the teachers who needed help with completing her university assignment. In my own (Holliday, 1991) doctoral study of university classrooms in Egypt, I found that I was not allowed to sit unobtrusively at the back of classrooms because the lecturers needed to treat me as a guest and have me sit at the front. In each of these cases it was what was revealed in researcher–subject relations that contributed to a deeper understanding of the nature of the culture in question.

It certainly became clear that ethical researcher behaviour, such as 'coming clean' or inviting 'collaboration', which are established in, for example, British educational settings, may not apply elsewhere, and are in themselves ethnocentric practices (Holliday, 2007: 149). Shamim (op cit) therefore finds that the teachers in her study are not prepared to 'collaborate' by checking through her classroom transcripts: they have more important things to do. An important implication of this is that researchers need to appreciate that what they have brought to the research setting is a way of thinking and talking about research—a researcher discourse—which may need to be seriously questioned if what may be a competing way of thinking and behaving within the research setting is to be taken seriously (Holliday, 2007: 140).

Another interesting example of arriving at the unexpected is Honarbin-Holliday's (2005) discovery that the taxi drivers, who took her back and forth to her research site at two university art departments in Tehran, while carrying out a study of art education, had a great deal of relevance to say to her. Their contribution provided her with an essential external dimension from which to see the issues in her study with fresh eyes (Holliday, 2007: 38).

Appreciating complexities

Returning to example 2, Duan began to think differently after his experience in the UK school and his conversations with the Chinese in the UK. He made an early strategic decision to begin by looking widely before focusing in on the research site in his quest of submission (Figure 1 [e]). He had to travel from the UK to China before arriving at the site of a secondary school in Wuhan. However, he began looking around for instances of social life that were relevant to his study on arrival in China—at the airport, on the train, in his sister's house where he stopped over on the way—taking note of conversations, observations and chance encounters. He felt that if the national university entrance examination had the sort of impact he suspected, then there would be evidence of this everywhere. He finally approached the students in his research setting via the sorts of conversations he had practiced while in the UK. In so doing he discovered 'private sites' in the diaries and personal stories they began to reveal to him. It was through this exploratory process that he arrived at an *emerging thesis*, which I have summarized in the left column of Figure 2.

Figure 2: Chinese student discourses

Take 1: Emerging thesis	Take 2: Further emerging thesis
There is a counter-discourse amongst students which is in conflict with a dominant discourse generated by parents, teachers and the media; and they do not wish to conform to the dominant 'examination' discourse. The students thus oppose the dominant idea that they are totally ruled by the examination process.	The student counter discourse contains within it elements of dominant discourse of parents within a yin-yang relationship.

Perhaps the best evidence that a researcher is sufficiently submitting to the emergent issues of the field is that ideas begin to move. This was certainly the case in Duan's study—even from the point of finding the unexpected in his first phase of conversational interviews. He moved significantly from the initial emergent thesis to a *further emerging thesis*, which I summarize in the right column of Figure 2. This further stage emerged because Duan did not rest with his initial phase of data collection, but returned to the site a year later to ask the students again. This persistent and continued effort to get to the bottom of things is a further measure of engaged and rigorous qualitative research.

I have expressed the two theses in the figure in terms of two *takes* on the same set of phenomena. It is important to note, however, that take 2 does not necessarily negate take 1: it can result in a more complex picture in which different *takes* represent different facets within an overall sense of greater complexity. Duan's initial thesis may therefore be possible some of the time within the scope of his second thesis. This fits well with the notion of yin and yang, which Duan describes as complementary opposites (2007: 247). This therefore represents a subtle movement away from the positivist desire to tie things down, and towards opening things up by achieving the greater richness necessary for thick description. In its complexity, his second emerging thesis possesses a verisimilitude—the convincing appearance of being true—because it adds to and incorporates his first. Discovering that the two discourses were present in each other made sense to the researcher because he had *personal knowledge* of this complexity in his own life. When thinking deeply, not as researchers, and about things not close to us, I believe that we actually know that things are very often far more complex than they initially seem. We are all able to assess what makes sense as long as we think in a disciplined way—and know our prejudices.

Detail and restraint

The persistent submission to the complexity of the data can also be seen in the way Duan addresses the detail of his data—and how it interconnects—which represents the ambivalence of real life. This can be seen in the following example from his discussion of data, where we see an extract from a student diary followed by Duan's analysis:

> I felt that Teacher Liang was a good teacher. The reasons for her to hit us or scold us were to nurture and educate us—to enable us to become useful, successful people. She did everything for our own good. (Diary 3.2, Bao Ling, 07/03/02)

This Teacher Liang is the same one that scolded Bao Ling in the first extract. It seemed that Bao Ling had already changed his view regarding this teacher. In the incident above, Bao Ling seemed to dislike the teacher. But in this extract, it seems that he tries to find some justification for his teacher's ill treatment of him, even defending his teacher for what she had done to him, showing his understanding of her having scolding him. This does not necessarily mean that he has changed his view. It may indicate consistently ambivalent feelings towards her. On the one hand, he hated his teacher for scolding him in public. On the other hand, he showed consent in witnessing his teacher's recital of the discourse. This may suggest that there might be traces or revelation or evidence of the dominant discourse within the students' discourse (Duan, 2007: 156–157)

In this discussion, Duan first of all exercises restraint from jumping too quickly into an interpretation. He sets the extract from the diary against another 'incident above' and uses this juxtaposition to move gradually from one possible interpretation to another.

The same complexity and ambivalence can be seen in this detailed description, from Herrera's dissertation, of the head-mistress at work, dealing with students in one of her classes:

Almost before she finished her sentence another student approached the desk, leaned forward placing her elbow at the edge of it, and with cast down eyes began to speak. The Headmistress screamed abruptly 'Stand up straight!! Now keep your arms at your sides!' The girl, flushed, continued to speak. (Herrera, 1992: 8)

As with Duan's diary extract, this small description cannot stand alone. Making sense of it depends on a complex set of relationships with other instances within the broader thick description. Nevertheless, even within this small piece of description, Herrera takes the time and care to immerse herself in the complexity of what is going on, almost as though she is allowing her own description of it to take on a life of its own. This is evident in the detailed noticing and recording of the student's posture and positioning of her eyes. The possible interpretation of what is going on in this event is not clear. The headmistress, from her scream, might simply be an authoritarian bully. On the other hand, the fact that the student dares put her elbow on her desk might indicate a tacit sensitivity and intimacy. Herrera goes for the latter, but only because of how this single instance connects with others.

Force of circumstance, writing, and resisting naivety

Once the researcher looks further and wider than the most obvious evidence and becomes open to greater complexity and richness, relevance can be found in the force of unexpected circumstance. Two incidental events made this very apparent to me. The first took place when I was attending a conference on qualitative research at Karachi University. Two takes on the same event are expressed in Figure 3.

Figure 3: The seat

Take 1: Self and Other	Take 2: People, politics and society
While standing outside one of the buildings of Karachi University a group of three young women students attending the same conference came up to me and asked questions about my presentation. I wanted to consult them about the dress codes of other young women students I had been watching while sitting on an empty seat in the central part of the university concourse. I asked them to come with me and sit in the same place so that I could show them. They agreed to come with me, but not to sit next to me on the still empty seat, where there was plenty of room for four people. My first take on this was that it was perhaps something to do with gender, age, cultural misunderstanding connected with 'a Muslim society'.	Later on I was walking in the same area with an older male lecturer from the same university. When I told him what had happened he explained that the seat I had chosen was usually occupied by students from a particular political party and that the students I had invited to sit there would not do so because they didn't want to be associated with the party. This explained why the seat was empty in the first place, even though the concourse was otherwise crowded with people. There was no-one from that particular political party around and no-one else would sit there. (I had presumed that when I had initially sat there no-one else had taken up the space next to me because they didn't want to sit with a foreigner.)

Of course the second take on why the women students would not sit down with me is not necessarily more accurate than take 1. It is not necessarily the case that the university lecturer who suggested this to me should know any better just because he was a lecturer at the same university. It would be too simplistic for me to presume that he knows better just because he is some sort of 'insider'. Culture is more complex than that. Just because I am a lecturer there does not mean that I understand what is going on between students on my university campus. Also, once again, take 2 does not necessarily negate take 1. As with Duan's two theses (Figure 2), both could be true at the same time. The political group factor may not have been sufficient in itself to deter the students from sitting on the seat with me, whose foreign presence may have been sufficient to have overridden it. Just because the political factor may have been ascendant at a particular time does not mean that it would continue to be so.

One reason for doubting the accuracy of take 2 is that it is certainly the case that I was drawn to it simply because it did provide *an* explanation, which was more reassuring than my general confusion in take 1. On the other hand, I cannot deny that there was an element of an Orientalist exoticizing of an 'Eastern', 'Muslim' culture in my perception of cultural difference in take 1. Against this, the university politics explanation of take 2 was far less Othering.

Something to note about the discipline of writing in take 1 is my choice of words, 'came up to me *and* asked'. The act of writing in itself makes me think more carefully about what was going on. I had to restrain myself as far as I could by writing, 'came up to me *to* ask', which would have presumed too much about their purpose which I could not know. Submission to detail can indeed be a significant mechanism whereby a researcher can acquire the 'stranger' viewpoint. Duan made detailed drawings of the way in which the pupils positioned themselves in his daughter's classroom (Figure 1[a]); and he returned to these again and again to gradually unravel what was going on. Grounds (2007), in her study of the nature of sustainability in university self access centres in Mexico, found that describing what she saw in detail enabled her to begin to move into a new viewpoint and to appreciate student behaviour in its own terms instead of in her own professional terms.

How naïve one can be about insider knowledge—the Pakistani lecturer just because he was Pakistani—was demonstrated to me in another incident while staying at a university hotel in Nanjing, in the two takes in Figure 4. Again, both takes could represent elements of truth; though what makes take 2 more believable is its complexity. The second one is based on further evidence, but does not negate take 1. It simply provides more layers of complexity.

Figure 4: Chinese breakfast

Take 1: Outsider to 'Chinese culture'	Take 2: Outsider behaviour everywhere
When on the first morning I went down for breakfast alone I found myself in a strange environment in which it was difficult for me to know how to proceed. On my right was a table with a large choice of different types of food. On my left was another table with a choice of large and small bowls and plates. I had no idea which type of food to put in or on which. As I hesitated a friendly English speaking Chinese person behind me very quickly told me what to do. On the second morning, after this guidance and after watching other people, I did better, helped myself, and sat down to eat.	After a short time I observed two Chinese people approaching the buffet—an older woman and a younger man—and, to my astonishment, they seemed, from the expressions on their faces, their hesitation and body language, to be just as much at a loss for what to do as I had been. Then I remembered how often one needs to enter into some sort of cultural learning when encountering yet another of the multiplicity of types of self-service cafés and restaurants one can find in 'native' Britain. It was not 'being Chinese' in 'Chinese culture' which would solve the problem, but just being familiar with a particular procedure.

Example 3: Egyptian university students

My third major example takes the issue of detail and complexity to another plane. It concerns a long-term revisiting of data collected as part of my own doctoral study of the curriculum politics of Egyptian university classrooms (Holliday, 1991), and concerns the photograph in Figure 5, which I took in 1988. The power of visual data of this sort is such that it carries a vast amount of cultural insinuation at a glance and can continue to have powerful meaning long after it was collected (Holliday, 2007: 66). This was certainly the case with this photograph. I have revisited it many times in my research and teaching to demonstrate a range of points, but it is only in recent years that I have seen something in it which I had ignored at the time when I took it. Take 1 in Figure 5 represents my original use of the image. It was instrumental in supporting my *professional* argument—that Egyptian students were not confined 'simply and passively' (in my terms at the time) to listening to lectures, but could also work more 'actively' (also in my terms) in groups.

Figure 5: Egyptian students

Take 1: Look what they can do because of us Evidence that the students were able to engage with innovation of working in groups in crowded classes	Take 2: Listen to what they really think 'This group work is really nothing very special at all. We can do this sort of thing very easily when we need to. Who are *you* [the English foreigner] to be making such a big deal out of it? And where is the theory?'

I had not really submitted myself to what the students had told me on several occasions, about how they felt about the classroom activities we were asking them to engage in. Even though the purpose of the research was to critique the ethnocentricity of the curriculum project as an 'importer' of Centre language teaching methodologies, I had not gone far enough into problematizing the dominant professional discourse. I had noted that Egyptian students and teachers did not lack the ability to master the new methodology and were able to make it their own, thus problematizing the need for foreign intervention; but I had not sufficiently critiqued the methodology itself. I had not been able to arrive at the far more undermining notion, expressed in take 2 in Figure 5, that the students, and indeed the teachers, might have had something far better to do than to engage with the new methodology and its implications.

What I understand much more now than I did then is the power of professional discourses in framing how we see the wider social world. The impact of critical discourse analysis in applied linguistics has been instrumental, in the last fifteen years, largely through the work of Normal Fairclough (e.g. 1995). Hence, doing my PhD at the same time as being an English language curriculum consultant, I was very much preoccupied with a powerful professional discourse. In Holliday (2005) I trace the manner in which this discourse constructs the picture of a 'non-native speaker' Other who is in need of cultural improvement in order to learn or teach English. I trace the roots of this discourse to the early days of an explicitly behaviouristic classroom method, and show how it has developed within a complex ideology of native-speakerism. My preoccupation was therefore with perceiving the students in the photograph as 'learners' who needed to be helped to adopt new strategies, rather than as people with their own views about education and society. Their comments in take 2 reflect not only their views about what was (in fact not) happening in the classroom, but their views about their relationship with the presence of foreign influence.

My understanding of this conflict was heightened by my analysis of one of my own qualitative descriptions of Hong Kong Chinese student classroom behaviour as part of a study of an English immersion programme in the UK in which they were students (Holliday, 2005: 31–2, 2007: 177). In Figure 6, take 1 is the original text of my description, and take 2 is my later realization of the ideology underpinning my writing of it. What I feel is important about this is that my later, reflexive excavation (take 2) of what I was doing in the field of study (take 1) actually comprises the more important finding.

Figure 6: Hong Kong Chinese students

Take 1: 'Childlike learners'	Take 2: Chauvinistic researcher
I was determined to get them into choosing topics for projects by the end of the morning…. The students arrived in dribs and drabs late. They arranged themselves around the cluster of tables fairly haphazardly. Some of them were beginning to turn on computers and I told them not to, to sit straight down—fearing that they were going to get onto their chat-lines. (I had got the impression previously that they spent every moment of 'free' time on chat lines)…. Then I left them for 30 minutes to devise ideas for projects…. When I returned they were remarkably on task. Some of them perkily looked round to say they were 'on-time'.	It may be difficult for the reader to see the traces of culturism here. I can because when I see what I wrote, it enables me to excavate the pre-occupations with a (to me) Other and unsatisfactory Chinese culture, which were there, but too deep for me to notice, at the time of writing. 'To get them' implies a superior teacher trying to change culturally 'inferior' behaviour of the object Other 'them' (rather than 'us'). 'Dribs and drabs', 'fairly haphazardly' and 'they…chat-lines' implies confirmation of this expected behaviour. 'Arranged themselves' implies a sense of degenerate self-indulgence—nothing better to do than to 'display' themselves 'ornamentally'. 'Get them…by…' also reveals the objectives-led control element of a so-called 'student-led' pedagogy within which students are in reality operatives to be 'improved' by a controlled treatment. Hence, I found it 'remarkable', on returning to the class after leaving to get something, to find that 'they' were actually doing the things I had set them—whereas there was no reason at all why they should not. Nevertheless, I still refer to them as being 'perky'—like 'children' rather than adult people.

In both of these cases from my own research, take 2 is the result not of further data within the setting itself, but of increased *personal knowledge* about the nature of professional discourses. Since I wrote my PhD thesis I have acquired a more mature personal knowledge of the politics of my profession and I was able to apply this knowledge to my writing in take 1 on the Hong Kong students.

Example 1 again: Locating the Egyptian girls' school within a sociological imagination

Returning to Herrera's study of the Egyptian girls' school, in the light of the other examples I have presented, what is it that gives validity to what she says about the headmistress, 'life, attitudes, struggles, relationships, confrontations, aspirations'. While the built up picture of her thick description is essential, what is also important is the distance she moves from the beginning to the end of her research experience. This is represented in the two takes in Figure 7, the first being her statement, at the beginning of her dissertation, about what led her to do the study in the first place, and the second being her final statement. She was drawn to the school by its exoticness, and there are certainly detailed descriptions of 'exotic' behaviour in the body of her dissertation— but it is the persistent working through of these experiences that enables her to come out in a very different place. She did not begin with a determination to find out what was common between two schools in Cairo and San Francisco with questions that she simply found answers for ('How far are the schools similar, in terms of a…, b…and so on') as in the first procedure in Figure 1. She posed the classic, general, ethnographic question, 'What is going on', but this question is special in that it leaves the route and procedures open.

Figure 7: Moving across worlds

Take 1: Approaching the strange	Take 2: Appreciating complexity
[a] loudspeaker…and the military-like responses of girls, drum beats and off-tune accordion blared into my room…. Irritation turned suddenly to fascination. 'What on earth are they doing over there?' I wondered. 'What are they saying? Who are they? What does it all mean?'…I wandered into the hall, still in pajamas, and asked an Arab student…what the ruckus was about. She…said, emphasizing the obviousness of it, 'It's a school'. A school. And yet its sounds were so unfamiliar. (Herrera, 1992: 6)	It is Egypt, it is the East, it is also a developing country. But it is also humanity. Beyond my initial fascination with the exotic protocol, drills, sounds and system, it became just an ordinary school. …I cannot count the times I felt myself transformed over six thousand miles and more than a decade away to the parochial school in downtown San Francisco that I attended as a child. Superficially the two schools are vastly different. …Yet despite their specific features [one can]…join them together in the world community of schools. (Herrera, 1992: 80–81)

Returning to the question I asked about Herrera's research at the beginning of the chapter—the basis upon which it can be established that what she claims is not just a product of her own imagination—has I think much to do with the distance she has moved from take 1 to take 2. This distance indicates that she has applied the disciplines of submission, emergence, and personal knowledge within the mechanisms of thick description.

Conclusion

To finish, I would like briefly to revisit the nature of the movement from take 1 to take 2 in the examples cited, and then relate this to the theme of decentred research. In each example a greater sense of validity is achieved because the researcher moves from an initial take on what is going on to a different, less expected position. This process is enabled by the disciplines of submission, emergence, and personal knowledge, and by thick description, whether it is as a result of revisitation, different viewpoints, different events or interventions, a new data collection technique, a new informant, or a mature understanding of the nature of things—a more mature personal knowledge. In each case the second take adds a dimension of complexity which does not necessarily negate the first take, but which certainly places it within a greater perspective of understanding.

The relationship between this ability to move into new realms of understanding is on the one hand a necessary ingredient of all good research. Certainly a very basic question to ask of doctoral candidates is 'what have you done to distance yourself from the familiar in such a way that the unexpected can begin to emerge?' On the other hand, decentred research requires this overthrowing of centred understandings and methodologies in perhaps more specific ways. Centred understandings conform to dominant, imagined notions of who people are and what they can do and what they should be allowed to do. In a postcolonial world, these unquestioned understandings have often serviced colonialism by depicting the foreign Other as culturally inadequate. In the examples of first takes in this chapter they include 'Chinese students are unthinkingly dominated by examinations' and 'Egyptian students need to be taught how to work in groups'. Centred methodologies are governed by unquestioned assumptions about the nature of relationships between researchers and their subjects and fail to stand outside professional and researcher discourses. It is not until these centred understandings are overthrown that there is any chance of understanding the Periphery cultural realities that remain obscured by Centre preoccupations.

I feel that an important implication of this is that decentred research is not a matter of *who* the researcher is, but of *how* they position themselves. Research into a Chinese community will not succeed just because the researcher is Chinese. Personal knowledge is not the same as insider knowledge of *what* a particular place or cultural reality is like; it is deeply reflected knowledge of *how* society, everywhere, works.

Bibliography

Bhabha, H., *The Location of Culture* (London: Routledge, 1994).

Clifford, J., 'Introduction: Partial Truths', in Clifford, J. and Marcus, G.E. (eds.), *Writing Culture: The Poetica of Politics of Ethnography* (Berkeley: University of California Press, 1986), 1–26.

Clifford, J., and Marcus, G.E. (eds.), *Writing Culture: The Poetica of Politics of Ethnography* (Berkeley: University of California Press, 1986).

Duane, Y., 'The Influence of the Chinese University Entrance Exam (English)', Ph.D. thesis (Department of English and Language Studies, Canterbury Christ Church University, 2007).

Fairclough, N., *Critical Discourse Analysis: The Critical Study of Language* (London: Addison Wesley Longman, 1995).

Faubion, J.D., 'Currents of Cultural Fieldwork', in P. Atkinson, A. Coffey, S. Delamont, J. Lofland, and L. Lofland (eds.), *Handbook of Ethnography* (London: Sage, 2001), 39–59.

Geertz, C., *The Interpretation of Cultures: Selected Essays* (London: Fontana, 1993).

Grounds, P., 'Discovering Dynamic Durability: Beyond Sustainability in an English Language Curriculum Project', Ph.D. thesis (English and Language Studies Department, Canterbury Christ Church University, 2007).

Guba, E.G., and Lincoln, Y.S., 'Paradigmatic Controversies, Contradictions, and Emerging Confluences', in N. K. Denzin, and Y. S. Lincoln (eds.), *Handbook of Qualitative Research*, 3e (Thousand Oaks, Ca: Sage Publications, 2005).

Gubrium, J.F., and Holstein, J.A., *The New Language of Qualitative Research* (New York: Oxford University Press, 1997).

Hammersley, M., and Atkinson, P., *Ethnography: Principles in Practice* (London: Routledge, 1995).

Herrera, L., 'Scenes of Schooling: Inside a Girls' School in Cairo', *Cairo Papers in Social Sciences*, 15 (1992) Monograph 1.

Holliday, A.R., 'Dealing with Tissue Rejection in EFL Projects: The Role of an Ethnographic Means Analysis', Ph.D. thesis (Department of Linguistics and Modern English Language, University of Lancaster, 1991).

Holliday, A.R., *Struggle to Teach English as an International Language* (Oxford: Oxford University Press, 2005).

Holliday, A.R., *Doing and Writing Qualitative Research*, 2e (London: Sage, 2007).

Honarbin-Holliday, M., 'Art Education, Identity, and Gender at Tehran and al Zahra Universities', Ph.D. thesis (Department of Art and Design, Canterbury: Christ Church University, 2005).

Lincoln, Y.S., and Guba, E.G., 'Paradigmatic Controversies, Contradictions, and Emerging Confluences', in N.K. Denzin, and Y.S. Lincoln (eds.), *A Handbook of Qualitative Research*, 2e (Thousand Oaks, CA: Sage, 2000), 163–188.

MacDonald, S., 'British Social Anthropology', in P. Atkinson, A. Coffey, S. Delamont, J. Lofland, and L. Lofland (eds.), *Handbook of Ethnography* (London: Sage, 2001), 60–79.

Schutz, A., 'The Stranger', *Collected Papers*, Vol. 2 (The Hague: Martinus Nijhoff, 1964), 91–95.

Shamim, F., *The Process of Research: A Socio-cultural Experience*, Unpublished paper, (Department of English, University of Karachi, 1996).

Spencer, J., 'Ethnography after Postmodernism', in P. Atkinson, A. Coffey, S. Delamont, J. Lofland, and L. Lofland (eds.), *Handbook of Ethnography* (London: Sage, 2001), 443–52.

Section II

Qualitative Research in the South:
Focus on Ethics

2

Ethical dilemmas in research with young children

A field experience from Pakistan

ALMINA PARDHAN

Introduction

In present times of a global network of communities and societies, educational research with young children in diverse socio-cultural contexts has resulted in researchers experiencing challenges to 'find ethically appropriate solutions' (Allen, 2005: 23) to dilemmas encountered in the field. Yet, as Greene and Hogan (2005) point out, it is only recently that a growing body of literature is emerging to address the complexity of methodological and ethical issues in relation to research with young children. This much needed literature has been important for novice educational researchers like me working with young children. Nevertheless, the current emerging body of knowledge in research with children assumes a predominantly ethnocentric universality as a defining measure by which to view social relations and practice (Dev Makkar, 2002). My research with children in the developing context of Pakistan where educational research with young children has only recently emerged (Pardhan and Juma, 2007; Vazir, 2004) illuminates a complex labyrinth of meanings within the research setting where ethical and moral codes governing social relations and practices hold different meanings than those currently being debated. Added to this complexity is that legislation governing research with children

in Pakistan—where the research culture itself is in its infancy—
is virtually non-existent and schools themselves have haphazard
policies regulating adult–child interactions. During my recent
doctoral research with young children in Pakistan, I therefore
continuously found myself grappling with many complex
practical and ethical issues, including those related to power
within adult–child research relationships. Dev Makkar (2002)
captures the tensions and dilemmas faced by researchers like
myself conducting research in diverse cultural and geographical
contexts:

> Apart from the obvious difficulty with distance, many obstacles arise
> from researching projects overseas, which the researcher is rarely
> prepared for. Studying to do research is never the same as actually
> doing it and although preparation is vital, it can never be adequate
> for the unpredictable, spontaneous events that mark research in the
> field as a unique experience. Our ethical and moral codes are too
> often challenged by the unexpected. We are placed in situations so
> specific, and sometimes so unforeseen, that it is often our judgment
> that becomes the most ready tool at such moments. This is not to
> say that the outcomes of these decisions is necessarily precarious,
> but that simply 'hands-on' research is really about the unknown.
> How our judgments are informed will therefore seriously affect how
> we seek out to investigate the research setting and ultimately how
> we view the results. (p. 75)

In this chapter I have used an account of my fieldwork carried
out for my doctoral dissertation in exploring how women
kindergarten teachers in Pakistan understand the concept of
gender as evident in their own reflections and teaching practice
with girls and boys to illustrate some of the ethical dilemmas I
encountered in my research with young children. Having lived
in four different continents—Africa, North America, Europe,
and South Asia—the geographical, cultural, religious, racial,
ethnic, linguistic, and class borders that I have crossed have
resulted in a constant tension between my insider and outsider
positions, particularly during my research in diverse cultural
contexts. I am a Shia Ismaili Muslim immigrant child of South

Asian origin born in Kenya. Much of my life has been spent in the Canadian context where I have pursued my education and my professional life as a teacher. At present, I am professionally situated in Pakistan as a teacher educator and educational researcher in the areas of early childhood education and gender. Nevertheless, I constantly traverse various countries. My socialization to teaching and educational research has largely been formed in the Canadian context. Most recently, I have pursued my doctoral studies through a Canadian university. Having conducted fieldwork for my master's thesis research on the experiences of women, schooling and work in a remote rural setting in Pakistan, I was keen to build upon this research both personally as well as for the potential contribution of this work to policy and practice in Pakistan and internationally. As such, field work for my doctoral study was also conducted in Pakistan.

During my doctoral fieldwork with young children in a Pakistani school, I struggled with applying conventional research ethics which governed the institutional setting of my foreign university. I often experienced tensions negotiating the contextual values and norms and the methodological needs and detachment suggested by applying conventional research ethics. Engaging in reflexivity was critical to explore and reflect upon my values, commitments and perspectives as well as my social and cultural position in relation to the research process (Glesne, 2006). Discussions with my colleagues at the recently established educational institute in Pakistan where I work, and where issues of implementing conventional research ethics in a developing context are being debated, were also important in helping me to make sense of the ethical dilemmas I encountered. Nonetheless, I found that I often had to trust my own understanding of the culture, my intuition, and my faith in God in making various research and ethical decisions in the different situations that arose in the field.

In this chapter, I present the tensions and dilemmas I encountered in my research with kindergarten children in

Pakistan as part of my doctoral dissertation. I open the chapter with a discussion by situating my own beliefs about children with notions of children and childhood in the context of Pakistan. Next, I present the process of negotiating my presence as an adult woman educational researcher and building a relationship of trust with the children in my study. A discussion on issues of consent and assent as well as negotiating research space for interviews in educational research with young children follows. Thereafter, I highlight some of the issues I faced in negotiating relationships with children not selected for the study sample. I conclude the chapter by offering suggestions based on my field experience in Pakistan to support researchers engaged in cross-cultural research to consider research ethics with children in diverse socio-cultural and geographical contexts.

The Research Context

My doctoral study was conducted over a period of one academic year in four kindergarten classrooms in a private, co-education, English-medium school in the urban city of Karachi, Pakistan. My research design featured mixed research methods comprising various qualitative and quantitative approaches to address my main research focus: how women kindergarten teachers in Pakistan understand the concept of gender evident from their own reflections and from their interaction with their female and male students. Within this research design, I observed the teachers' teaching practice and interactions with all the students in their classrooms and then, more specifically, with sixteen target children—eight girls and eight boys. I interviewed the sixteen target children to get insight into their perceptions of their teachers' teaching practice and interaction with them regarding gender. The sixteen target children's gendered interactions with peers in school were also observed and the mothers of these children were interviewed about their gender beliefs and practices raising their children.

In the remaining sections of this chapter I sketch the complex ethical issues of conducting my research specifically with the kindergarten children in a setting which is only recently beginning to see a gradual emergence of educational research activity with young children (Pardhan and Juma, 2007; Vazir, 2004). I present the dilemmas of respecting the ethical considerations of my Canadian university and the general social science community as well as the local standards of conduct and ethics—considerations which often became blurred (Dev Makkar, 2002). Emond (2005) has argued about the importance of a reflexive approach when reading about accounts of research with young children. As such, I begin by situating myself as a researcher in the Pakistani context and negotiating my beliefs about children with notions of children and childhood in Pakistan.

Negotiating my beliefs about children with notions of children and childhood in Pakistan

In the recent literature which has begun to explore methodological issues with children in the developed contexts, it has been argued that 'the predominant emphasis has been on children as objects rather than children as subjects, on child-related outcomes rather than child-related process and on child variables rather than children as persons (Greene & Hill, 2005: 1). Greene and Hill (2005: 3) further note that, 'Children in most societies are valued for their potential and for what they will grow up to be but are devalued in terms of their present perspectives and experiences.' In many parts of the world, including South Asian countries like Pakistan, children's voices are generally not heard; children are usually expected to listen to and obey their elders; questioning or challenging their elders' decisions is considered culturally inappropriate and usually frowned upon; young children are considered immature and are often referred to as 'empty slates' (Vazir, 2007). Through my research and teaching in early childhood education in Pakistan, I am aware of the challenges that arise in schools and at home when children are encouraged to think critically and raise questions in classrooms which go against cultural beliefs and beliefs about the process of education.

In my own South Asian cultural upbringing, I have experienced such tensions in my relationship with elders. Through my parents, my extended family and my community, an important value that has been transmitted is respecting and obeying our elders. Such views of elders were also part of the greater cultural and education fabric of Kenya while I was growing up. Both my parents are educators. As such, my home environment and my interactions with my parents provided me with many opportunities for exploring and asking questions. Nevertheless, I was aware of certain boundaries. My largely teacher-directed, textbook driven formal education in Kenya rarely provided me with opportunities to ask questions or to think critically. Asking questions and challenging a teacher's authority were often discouraged with reprimands.

Consequently, adjusting to the cultural and education fabric of Canada in the early eighties as an immigrant student was difficult. My teachers expected me to ask questions. I observed my peers fearlessly asking questions and, at times, challenging our teachers. All of this seemed very peculiar and sometimes alarming to me. A large part of my eventual adjustment in the Canadian school system was due to my parents' support. Being educators and having received their post secondary education in Europe, they understood the Canadian school system and helped me to adjust. Yet, it was never completely without tension.

Over the past few years, my research and teaching in early childhood education and my experiences as a mother of two young children have contributed to my view of children and childhood. In Canada, I had opted to teach older children and adolescents. At the time, I felt that teaching young children would be overwhelming and challenging. My view was that young children knew little and needed to be taught everything. When I had my own children and began to work in the area of early childhood education, I realized the limitation of my views. I came to see '(Young) children, through their talk and interaction, as participating actively in the construction of their social situations' (Danby and Farrell, 2004: 36). I realized children bring with them a wealth of prior knowledge from their life experiences into the classroom.

Having been raised with similar cultural values and traditions that are found in Pakistan and having worked with teachers in this context, I had some understanding of the position of children in relation to adults. This raised important implications for me as a researcher in this setting—the rapport that I created with the children, the way I spoke with them, the way I framed my questions, the way I created a space for them to share their experiences. Nevertheless, I constantly found myself negotiating: the conventional research ethics of my foreign university; my own understanding of research and teaching largely informed from a Canadian perspective; and the ethical and moral standards of conduct within the research setting.

Negotiating adult–child relationships in the field

The process of establishing rapport with the children also brought with it many dilemmas that I had not anticipated. Various tensions related to my multiple identities, particularly my position as an 'adult woman', arose as I negotiated my presence with the children. Within this cultural context, I was conscious of the way culture and gender added to the complexity of establishing rapport with the children (Holmes, 1998). Negotiating my role as an 'adult woman' amongst other adults in the school environment with the status of ability and power was often challenging. This power was particularly associated to my role as an 'adult nurturer' and an 'adult with formal authority' (Greene and Hill, 2005; Hill, 2005; Holmes, 1998). My predominantly Canadian frame of reference in relation to ethics in research and teaching added to the complexity. Mayall (2000) has argued that the subordinate position of the child cannot be ignored in relation to the adult researcher and, therefore, must be taken into account by the researcher. In this section, I elaborate upon how I negotiated my adult presence with the children in my study in my attempt to ensure an ethical research.

Negotiating my presence as an 'adult woman' researcher

I entered into the field giving little consideration that the simple act of a child addressing me would become a source of tension in the research process. Working as an adult in educational settings in the Canadian context, I am used to being formally addressed as 'Ms Pardhan' by my students. In my introduction to the children for my fieldwork in a Pakistani school, the children were guided by their teachers to address me as 'Almina Aunty': A culturally appropriate form of address for a woman, but which I began to perceive as problematic in terms of children's perceptions of my role in their classrooms and school. The kindergarten teachers themselves were also referred to by the students as 'Aunty' or the teacher's first name with 'Aunty' affixed at the end, i.e. 'Azra Aunty'[1]. This is a normal occurrence in most early years' settings in Pakistan. It is also common practice in this cultural setting where adults within a family or who have close relations with a family are referred to as 'Aunty' and 'Uncle' by young children as a sign of respect. Even adults who may not be familiar to children, such as an elderly shopkeeper, may be referred to as 'Uncle' or 'Aunty'. This South Asian cultural practice is one with which I have also grown up. Nevertheless, as a researcher used to the distance created by the more formal ways of being addressed by my students in Canadian schools, I found that negotiating my relationship through the familial address 'Aunty' created multiple tensions during the research process. While the title 'Aunty' facilitated more trusting relationships with the children, it also blurred the boundaries of the kind of detachment suggested by applying conventional research ethics and which may have been easier to maintain by being more formally addressed.

Over the course of the field work, I became an 'Aunty' who participated in nearly all of their school activities. Unbeknownst to the children, my prior association with the school as a teacher educator whom the staff held with high regard and trust brought with it a dimension that would influence the children's relationship with me. Everyday, the children would observe their teachers and administrative staff greeting me with a warm embrace as is common cultural practice and interacting with me throughout the day in collegial, warm and respectful ways. I also had the privilege of interacting in all the spaces that the children and their teachers occupied at the school. Over the course of the year, the children also observed my interactions with their parents, most of whom accorded me trust and respect as an 'expert' in the field of education. I was an 'Aunty' whom their teachers, administrative staff and parents trusted.

In the children's eyes, my physical appearance was also just like one of the 'Aunties' they might interact with in their daily lives. My brown skin color and shoulder-length, dark hair made me look like their teachers and other women in their lives. I was Muslim like their 'Aunties'. I ate similar food as they did. Just as I had during my research experience in northern Pakistan, I also followed the local dress code of wearing *shalwar kameez*[2] (Pardhan, 2007). While I did not cover my head as their teachers were required to do, I nevertheless felt that my attire made me look just like any Pakistani woman the children would see in their environment. In this cultural context, it is normal for children to see women who either cover or do not cover their heads interacting with one another. In my research site, where children were expected to communicate in English and where teachers spoke in English, my limited proficiency in Urdu which would have made my 'outsider' status more evident was made almost invisible. From a very young age, I have learned 'accent-switching' when I speak English—and I do this unconsciously. Growing up in Canada, I have been able to switch between Canadian and South Asian accents when I speak English. This has been an important skill for being accepted amongst diverse groups with whom I interact. As such, I was able to speak English in an accent similar to the teachers and the children at the school.

Tensions being perceived as nurturer

During the course of my fieldwork, I became conscious that the title 'Aunty' brought with it tensions in relation to children's expectations that I perform nurturing and caregiving acts. The title 'Aunty', a family term, carries with it roles and expectations one of which includes 'nurturer'. Within the patriarchal extended family structures in the context of Pakistan, young children look up to adult female family members for nurturing and caregiving support. The title 'Aunty' for teachers of young children suggests a more personal relationship with them as an extension of the extended family system into early years' educational settings. This has implications on children's expectations of their female teachers in terms of their caring and nurturing roles. Holmes (1998) has pointed out that one of the multiple roles of predominantly female nursery school and kindergarten teachers is substitute mother with caring and nurturing roles. I feel that in the context of Pakistan this is made even further complex by the family relationship embedded within the title 'Aunty'.

In the formal web of relations of the school environment where the kindergarten teachers were also 'Aunty', I was aware that being an 'adult woman' and being called 'Aunty' presented a closer proximity to the children's teachers. Many children classified me in a similar way as their teachers expecting nurturing and care giving acts. Even when their own classroom teachers were present, I found myself approached by young children to perform care giving acts which I had observed their teachers performing. Like their teachers, I was asked by children to: tie laces; button shirts; tuck shirts into shorts; open water bottles and lunch boxes; help put on hair ornaments; zip backpacks; and arrange material in their backpacks. I found this very endearing and I would help the children. Being a mother of very young children made my reaction to help them spontaneous. However, I found such requests problematic during my formal timed observations. If I noticed that their teachers were around and not occupied in other tasks, I directed the children to their teachers. Otherwise, I helped the children and made a note in my observation records of this. Like Holmes (1998) in her research with children, I felt that these experiences and interactions with the children strengthened our relationship by facilitating the development of mutual trust and security during interviews with and observations of children. Nevertheless, it made me reflect upon children's gender socialization as well as their perceptions of female and male roles and responsibilities through their classroom interactions with their kindergarten teachers and me, a female researcher.

Tensions being perceived as adult with formal authority

Being addressed as 'Aunty' also brought with it tensions in relation to children's perceptions of my role as an 'adult with formal authority'. My particular situation doing research in Pakistan where I was addressed as 'Aunty' further complicated this. Research with children involves the fundamental issue of adults' power and authority in relation to children's powerlessness. Within the Pakistani context, this dichotomy is particularly apparent (Behera, 2007; Vazir, 2007). Like Thorne (1993) in her research with children, I found that my greater size, access to spatial relations with other adults at school, and my status as adult in an educational setting drew 'sharp generational divisions' (p. 16) and 'mark(ed) them with differences in authority and power' (p. 16). However, I also found that cultural norms governing adult-child relationships within this context added to the complexity. An assumption lying within the familial address 'Aunty' is that of a caring, nurturing woman who might find it difficult to discipline children. Yet, within this cultural context, authoritarian forms of discipline which include scolding and spanking are part of the norm within homes and extending into the school system. While problematic, such forms of discipline viewed from this cultural perspective are often indicative of adult affection and love towards a child. Although, spanking/hitting children was prohibited at the school where I conducted field work, teachers did scold children. In fact, one of my women teachers, a research participant, even commented that an aspect of teaching which she enjoys is 'scolding' children in the sense of affectionately facilitating their development.

During my initial days of observations, I was not very conscious of the 'adult authority' role that I brought with me to the research setting. With multiple dimensions involved in the research process, I was still trying to make sense of handling data collection. I started becoming more aware of my position as 'adult with formal authority' when children sought permission to drink water or go to the washroom as well as support to resolve conflicts amongst themselves. Like Thorne (1993), I wanted to avoid being seen as an authority figure disciplining children and telling them what they could and could not do, knowing how sensitive children are to adults' actions. It was critical for me not to place myself in any situation which would jeopardize the children, the teachers or my position at the school. I wanted to be careful that the children did not perceive me taking sides with some children and not others. I needed the children to develop a positive relationship of trust with me. This was especially important as one of the phases of my study included interviewing cases of children. Like Vazir (2004) in her research with children in Pakistan, I 'resolved to be continually aware of the potential implications of how I acted and spoke' (p. 173). And just as Thorne (1993) attempted to negotiate her way through her research with children, I too began to avoid positions of authority and rarely intervened in a managerial way. Unless physical injury was at stake or a child's feelings were being hurt and there was no teacher nearby, I did not get involved in children's disputes. I even carefully calculated where I positioned myself to record my observations in the classroom. I was aware that where I sat in relation to the teachers could influence how the children perceived me. While it was not always possible to be seated away from the teacher, I tried my best to ensure this. However, as Thorne describes in her chapter, 'Learning from kids' in *Gender Play* (1993), negotiating a role of 'least adult' continued to be complicated and challenging.

I perceived that my evolving relationship of trust with the teachers also created tensions in the way children viewed me. Sometimes the teachers asked me to read stories to the children. Though I complied with their requests, I was cognizant that this had implications on my researcher role. I sensed that it created both a relationship of trust with the children and brought to fore my adult status. This was particularly evident when classroom management issues arose during storytelling which I was careful to avoid and to defer to the teacher. On a few occasions, I perceived that a few teachers assumed I was a colleague who would back up their rule. Sometimes they would ask me to keep an eye on the children if they had to leave the room. Towards the end of the year, one teacher even left the classroom while I was there without telling me she was going. These situations were problematic and created dilemmas for me. On the one hand, I was aware of the implications of being alone with the children; on the other hand, it was very awkward for me to say 'no' or discuss these tensions with the teachers. My Canadian teacher training had conditioned me to be wary of potential legal issues that could arise with students especially in a classroom not assigned to you for teaching. Moreover, I was concerned about incidences that might arise where I might be expected to engage in authoritarian forms of discipline appropriate in this cultural context, but problematic from my frame of reference. Yet, in this context the cultural appropriateness of the situation where young children's security in the hands of females is an understood norm presented little concern. I wondered if it would be appropriate to raise my concerns about this with the teachers. I felt that my relationship of trust with the teachers and the school might be compromised if I brought up my concerns. I, therefore, agreed to be alone with the children in the classroom when the teacher had to take care of other matters—but not without saying a small prayer that nothing wrong would happen!

Negotiating tensions of proximity and physical contact with children

Two issues which I grappled with throughout the research process as I established my relationship with the children were proximity to and physical contact with children. I often felt caught between my Canadian framework of space and interaction with children and what I learned during my fieldwork to be a norm in the context of Pakistan. My socialization to teaching and research with children from a largely Canadian perspective has taught me to keep my distance with children. Yet, I began to notice how close the children would come to me during my fieldwork. This caused me some discomfort and alarm. Initially I tended to pull back. As I observed children interacting with their teachers, I became aware of the physical contact between them: teachers would hold children close to them; teachers would ruffle children's hair, tickle them under their chins, pinch their cheeks affectionately, and touch their head, shoulder or back gently; children would stand or sit very close to their teachers; teachers would hug children who were feeling sad or who were hurt. From my own experiences as an early childhood education teacher educator, I also knew how important touch is for young children. Although I found myself intuitively beginning to close the gap between the children and me, I remained somewhat unsettled as to its appropriateness from a research perspective. When I shared my dilemma with some of my colleagues at the educational institution in Pakistan where I work, I learned that in this cultural context proximity and physical contact is common behavior amongst teachers and young children. While I made a more conscious effort to accommodate the local culture's framework of proximity and physical contact with children in school, it was nevertheless a constant struggle for me to break free of my conditioned behavior of remaining distant towards children in educational settings.

Negotiating the Interview Process with Children

Interviewing young children for my research was also fraught with contextually related tensions that I was unable to anticipate prior to beginning the process. Two critical dilemmas I encountered were negotiating the research space and negotiating relationships with those children not selected for the interview sample.

Negotiating Research Space for the Interviews with Children

Doing research with children in a Pakistani school in compliance with an ethical protocol from my foreign university brought with it tensions in relation to ethics and physical research space according to local standards and norms. Dockett and Perry (2007) describe the physical aspects of research space as being those locations in a child's school environment that are comfortable and familiar to children; in these locations, there is relative ease of movement into and out of the research space for children. In more developed contexts increasing governance around research with children in schools has implications on physical research space. Danby and Farrell (2004) have argued that legislation, policies and practices developed by adults for children's protection present challenges for educational research. For example, in Britain researchers are generally not allowed to be alone with an individual child (Hill, 2005). When discussing where I would interview children for my study, my supervisor had advised that it be done in the classroom during teaching-learning time.

However, the existing socio-cultural circumstances in this context entailed a different code of conduct. As such, my negotiation of the physical aspects of research space with children in a Pakistani school took on a different meaning. Because of my prior association as a teacher educator with the school and the relationship of trust I had developed through my research with the kindergarten teachers, I was given the privilege to interact with children on the school premises in much the same way as the other teachers. This privilege also extended to situations of being alone with individual children.

As part of my ethical protocol, I had anticipated conducting interviews with children in the classroom. However, this was problematic. From my Canadian frame of reference, the classroom was smaller than I had anticipated and had no space conducive to interview children. I was also aware that other children would become curious and might not focus on their class work or they may come to the research space out of curiosity. In this particular context where notions of individual space and privacy hold a different meaning than I have experienced in Canada, I felt that interviewing children in their classroom would therefore be problematic. I was reminded of my experiences in Booni Valley, Pakistan, conducting fieldwork for my master's thesis with the local women:

> When I conducted interviews in Canada, I had always experienced privacy between the participant and myself. I had anticipated this to be the case in Booni Valley as well. However, within this cultural context it was part of life to have many people present and I had to work around this. For example, some young women would be looking after their children during the interview; others would be feeding their children; others would be cooking.
>
> Members of the household were fascinated by my presence and by the audio equipment I had brought with me to record the interviews. I often had to be on the lookout for young children who were curious and wanted to touch my tape recorder during the recording of interviews. In some instances, there were constant interruptions as family members wanted to come in to meet me. It was a very fascinating experience for me. There were times when I felt that the interviews took longer because of this, but I had to respect their interest in me. (Pardhan, 2007: 250–251)

Nevertheless, I knew that the children needed to be in an environment where the space, material and people were familiar to them (Hill, 2005). Having taught in Canada and being a doctoral student at a Canadian University, I entered the field with the understanding that I could not be alone with any individual child. In his discussion on research ethics with young children in the West, Hill (2005, p. 73) writes,

> With current high public consciousness about risk and child protection, many would have qualms about the potential for children in such circumstances to be initiated into abuse. The risk of exploitation exists in any context where an adult researcher is alone with a child. Commonly, researchers are not allowed to be alone with an individual child in schools.

As such, I had to negotiate an appropriate and ethical research space to interview the children.

I conducted some interviews in the library, a large space in the school, when the class had their library period. With the teachers' permission, I also conducted a number of the interviews in the kindergarten resource room which was used daily by all the kindergarten teachers with small groups of students. This space was familiar to the children and, with only a few children and a teacher in the room at a time, it was possible to find a corner to talk with them. The teachers supported my use of this space from the perspective of children's comfort and classroom management. I explained to the teachers that I would first ask the children if they were comfortable to be in the resource room with me. If any child said 'no' or showed any sign of discomfort, I would not take them there. Even if a child agreed to come to the resource room and during the interview began to feel uncomfortable, I would bring them back to the classroom. In the event that I had to interview the child in the classroom, I indicated that I would work around the teachers' schedule such that it did not become a distraction for the other children. As it turned out, none of the children showed concern to be interviewed in the resource room.

On one occasion, the resource room was unavailable which became problematic. The child asked if we could go to the play area some distance away from the kindergarten section. This space was comfortable and familiar to this girl and she could easily leave this 'research space' and return to her classroom at anytime (Dockett and Perry, 2007). My own orientation of being a student and a teacher in Canada raised alarm bells about being alone with the child in this area. If I said 'no', how would the child feel? What if she asked why? Would it make sense to her if I said that I could not be alone with her? By this time she had come to see me as someone she trusted and who was part of her school environment. In her school, teachers and support staff like *maasis*[3] would often be alone with an individual child in different spaces. I suggested we ask her teacher what we should do.

The young girl ran ahead of me to ask her teacher before I could. Her teacher smiled happily saying it would be no problem. I panicked. What should I do? What if there were no other children or teachers around. If I shared my alarm with the teacher how would she react? My multiple identities of teacher educator and 'guest' in the school lent themselves to my being accorded great trust and respect by the teachers. Moreover, the idea of teachers being alone with an individual child did not appear to be an issue in this school. At that moment, I decided to follow what appeared to be culturally appropriate. I agreed to the girl that we have the interview in this area. When we arrived there, I was, nonetheless, relieved to see other children and teachers for a physical education lesson in the ground nearby.

The multiple identities that I brought to the research setting, particularly that of teacher educator and individual perceived as having 'expertise' in early childhood education placed me in both privileged and precarious positions. While it was often problematic for me to negotiate the tensions I experienced in such situations, my position of privilege allowed me to carry on with my research. There were moments when I pondered over the course that my fieldwork might have taken had I been limited in my movements in the school and in the spaces where I could interact with children. Moreover, I often felt burdened by the onus placed on me of my ethical conduct during my fieldwork given my position of privilege. Not only did I have to take care that no harm came to children from a research point of view, but I also had to make sure that I honor the trust placed in me by the school staff.

Negotiating my relationship with children not selected as a sample for my study

Much of the focus on conventional research ethics is ensuring the privacy and protection of individuals giving informed consent to participate in the research. In the case of research with children, ethical protocols of foreign universities like mine require parental consent and child assent to which I adhered. What is often not discussed at any great length, particularly in research with children, is the negotiating of relationships with those children not selected as part of a study sample. In the context of Pakistan, where research with children is a relatively new phenomenon, and adult-child relationships hold a different meaning than in more developed contexts, I found it problematic to deal with this complex issue. Negotiating relationships with those children not selected for interviews and peer observations was one of the most difficult experiences I encountered.

In my initial assent to all the kindergarten children when I began classroom observations of teachers, practice and interaction with their entire class, I had indicated that I would only be able to talk to a few of them individually. Nevertheless, this seemed to make little difference for many of the children. When I began my interviews with the 16 target children, other children would inquire why I was only talking to a few of them and if they too could be part of the process. I had not anticipated this. I realized that the way I framed my responses to the non-sample children had cultural implications. As discussed earlier, I had come to be seen as a trusted adult through my relationships with the kindergarten children's teachers and parents. While my adult woman status made me like their teachers, participating with children in the classroom in ways that were different than other adults in the school also made me different from their teachers. Furthermore, the children sensed my position of privilege at the school and the respect accorded to me by staff and parents as an 'outsider with expert knowledge and experience'. In the children's eyes, I was as a 'special' person whom they all wanted to be around. It was important, therefore, that I not hurt their feelings nor jeopardize their trust in me. I was also concerned about possible implications of telling them that their parents had not given consent for their participation. I was uncertain if they would understand the notion of parental consent in relation to conventional research ethics. Moreover, I was concerned about parent-child relationships, particularly given cultural norms of respecting elders and more authoritarian forms of child-rearing practices, if I told the children that their parents had not given permission for me to talk with them individually about their experiences. I, therefore, chose to explain to non-sample children who approached me that I only had time to speak with a few of them alone. I also mentioned that I was interested in talking with them and that I would come when they were playing or eating their snack which I did. I was very grateful for the flexibility and freedom that allowed me to move seamlessly from one class to another. It allowed me to spend time thereby having some form of interaction with all the children. Some children also wanted to use the crayons and play dough that they had seen the sample children use during the interview process. I received permission from the teachers to give all the children paper and crayons to use after they had completed their work. The children were delighted about this.

In a few instances, I interviewed mothers and children at their home. This also complicated matters. The children in my sample would excitedly tell their peers when I had been to their homes. The non-sample children would come and ask if I could visit their homes as well. On one occasion, a boy came running to me after his friend had told him I had been to his house. He invited me to his home, giving me precise directions to get there. In this culture being a guest in someone's home is greatly valued. Great preparations are involved when hosting someone. Moreover, when families host someone who is perceived to be very important their own prestige is raised. I told the young boy that

I would check if it would be possible to come, being fully aware that it would be impossible for me to go. This was a very painful thing to do knowing that it would have ethical implications on the research process. I wished that I could have accommodated the requests of children to come to their homes knowing what meaning and significance such events have.

On another occasion, a mother approached and asked if there was something wrong with her daughter. I was puzzled by her remark and inquired what she meant. She elaborated saying that her daughter had told her, 'Almina Aunty doesn't talk to me anymore.' Upon reflection, I realized that I had just begun my interviews and observations of the target children's peer interactions. I shared this with the mother and told her that I would try to make sure that I had some interaction with her daughter whenever I was in her classroom which her mother greatly appreciated. This led me to wonder how many other children felt the same way. Through my experiences of living in this context, I have learned that Pakistani parents generally expect people with whom they have established a relationship of trust to talk with their child and/or to pat their child affectionately on the head, cheeks, arms or back. Otherwise, they feel that something may be wrong with their child. Initially I was quite surprised as this challenged my frame of reference of what I had learned and experienced living and teaching in Canada. Behera (2007) has also pointed out that children living in South Asia are exposed to a system of social values, ethos and cultural patterns that are substantially different from Western values and ethos. South Asian children grow up in a society which focuses on the cultural identities of the communities rather than on eurocentric values of individualism (Goonesekere, 1997; Behera, 2007).

Discussion

In this chapter, I have explored ethical dilemmas in conducting research with children in Pakistan as part of my doctoral study. These dilemmas arose through my insider/outsider position in the developing context of Pakistan where current conventional research ethics of my Canadian university which assume an ethnocentric universality often seemed contradictory and culturally inappropriate. My experiences were rendered further complex by the virtually non-existent legislation governing research with children in Pakistan and by haphazard policies regulating adult-child interactions in Pakistani schools. While the growing body of literature is a timely response to the debate around complexities of research ethics with children, a vacuum is still evident in dealing with complex ethical issues arising from research with children in diverse geographical settings like Pakistan. This in itself made it all the more challenging for me in my research with children in Pakistan. Engaging in reflexivity throughout the research process was, therefore, critical for me to explore and negotiate both my own presentation of 'adult' self in research with children as well as the various ethical and moral forms of conduct required in the cultural context of a school in Pakistan.

Ethical dilemmas around adult-child relationships discussed in developed world contexts (Holmes, 1998; Thorne, 1993) have some applicability in a context like Pakistan. Yet, as I experienced it, differences in the construction and perception of such relationships by adults and children in diverse cultural contexts have implications on the research process. This was particularly evident in the way I was addressed as 'Aunty' by children which influenced children's perceptions of my status as 'adult woman researcher'. I was seen to hold dual roles of 'adult nurturer' and 'adult with formal authority' which complicated the researcher role I assumed I would have in the field. My features which clearly identify me to be of South Asian origin and my Muslim identity added to this complexity in the way children categorized me in relation to other adults at their school. At the same time, my outsider position being from Canada and my perceived expertise in early childhood education placed me in a privileged position with the status of an honored 'guest' in the school. This, in turn, made the research process problematic in negotiating relationships with both the sample and non-sample children during my fieldwork who were eager for my attention and affection.

Current literature exploring ethics in research space with children (Dockett and Perry, 2007) has also been valuable in considering ethical issues in research with children in contexts like Pakistan. Nevertheless, as I experienced through my field work in Pakistan, local standards governing relationships with children make issues of research space as discussed from the perspective of more developed countries problematic. As another of the children's 'Aunties' in the school, I found myself straddled between observing local cultural norms, the ethical protocol of my foreign university as well as conventional ethics in research with children. As I negotiated research space with children and proximity and touch in my relationships with children, I often found myself positioning myself towards local standards which seemed more ethically appropriate. This was not without discomfort given the strong influence of my Canadian framework about adult relationships with children in educational settings. Nevertheless, I was always careful not to lose sight of my research agenda nor manipulate the research process such that harm befell any children.

My experiences of carrying out research with children in Pakistan further point to the fundamental need for adults to suspend notions of childhood which render children voiceless, invisible and powerless thereby marginalizing them (Dockett & Perry, 2007; Emond, 2005; Vazir, 2004). Rather this chapter has recognized children as competent, capable and active participants in the research process whose meaningful participation may be facilitated through the use of particular protocols and practices (Dockett & Perry, 2007) which take into consideration ethical and moral codes governing social relations and practices within diverse cultural settings (Dev Makkar, 2002). Furthermore, it has highlighted the importance of contextualizing research to better understand children's experiences of the world and to grant them "their rightful position as 'expert'" (Emond, 2005:

136). Children's views and experiences need to be heard and respected in a research process which empowers them to have control over their involvement and over how researchers are included in their interactions, including the time and speed at which researchers are invited into their world (Emond, 2005). As such, research with children is a multi-layered process requiring the formation of relationships of trust between the adult researcher and the child as well as the on-going negotiation of children's involvement.

However, in order to ensure that children from diverse cultural and geographic settings are heard and respected in the research process, my research suggests the reconsideration of current conventional research ethics which assume an ethnocentric universality to one which creates space for contextually relevant ethical and moral codes of conduct. Educational institutions around the world, particularly developing countries like Pakistan, can play a critical role in bringing forward this debate and influencing current policies governing research ethics which stem from a developed country perspective. Educational institutions can also prepare novice researchers like me who engage in cross-cultural research with children through courses and workshops which focus on ethical codes of conduct in diverse geographical settings, including the developing context and how researchers might negotiate their insider/outsider positions. At a national level, legislation governing research with children in Pakistan and more uniform policies regulating adult-child relationships which protect young children are also critical. My research with children in Pakistan as both insider and outsider has highlighted the important role of reflexivity in making transparent the research process such that the researcher's own values, commitments and perspectives are considered. This is particularly critical in ensuring researcher responsibility in an ethical research process.

In closing, this chapter has been significant in raising complex ethical issues that arise in field work in a cultural context where current ethnocentric standards governing ethics in research cannot be imposed piecemeal. We live in an exciting time in the research community where crossing geographical borders has immense potential to develop insights into experiences of young children around the world to enhance their learning and development. As educational researchers, we therefore have a responsibility to adopt ethical approaches in our research with children who consider and respect social relations and practices within diverse cultural contexts to ensure children's protection and well-being.

Notes

1. A pseudonym.
2. The *kameez* is a loose fitting shirt and the *shalwar* is a pair of baggy trousers. These pieces are complemented with a *dupatta*—a long scarf.
3. In some South Asian dialects, the word '*maasi*' is used to address a mother's sister. In Urdu, one of Pakistan's two national languages, however, the word '*khala*' has the same meaning and is used to address a mother's sister. In the Pakistan context, the word '*maasi*' is often used to refer to female domestic help either in the home or school. In schools, *maasis* are employed as part of the support staff to provide assistance to very young children. Some of their responsibilities are to help children use the washroom, wash their hands, tie their laces, or open water bottles. *Maasis* are also responsible for: cleaning like dusting and mopping; making tea; and helping teachers prepare their resource material. Most middle and upper class private and community schools have *maasis*. Public schools also have *maasis*, but experience challenges retaining them on a daily basis.

References

Allen, G., 'Research Ethics in a Culture of Risk', in A. Farrell (ed.), *Ethical Research with Children* (Berkshire, UK: Open University Press, 2005), 15–26.

Behera, D.K., 'Introduction', in D.K. Behera (ed.), *Childhoods in South Asia* (New Delhi, India: Pearson Longman, 2007), 1–25.

Danby, S., and Farrell, A., 'Accounting for Young Children's Competence in Educational Research: New Perspectives on Research Ethics', *Australian Educational Researcher*, 31(3) (2004), 35–49.

Dev Makkar, B., 'Roles and Responsibilities in Researching Poor Women in Brazil', in T. Welland and L. Pugsley (eds.), *Ethical Dilemmas in Qualitative Research* (Hants, England: Ashgate Publishing Limited, 2002), 75–93.

Dockett, S., and Perry, B., 'Trusting Children's Accounts in Research', *Journal of Early Childhood Research*, 5(1) (2007), 47–63.

Emond, R., 'Ethnographic Research Methods with Children and Young People' in S. Greene and D. Hogan (eds.), *Researching Children's Experiences Methods and Approaches* (London, UK: Sage, 2005), 123–139.

Glesne, C., *Becoming Qualitative Researchers: An Introduction*, 3e (Boston, MA: Pearson Education, Inc., 2006).

Goonesekere, S., 'A Regional Response to Children's Rights in Asia: Problems and Prospects', in E. Verhellen (ed.), *Understanding Children's Rights* (Gent: Children's Rights Center, University of Ghent, 1997).

Greene, S., and Hill, M., 'Researching Children's Experience: Methods and Methodological Issues', in S. Greene and D. Hogan (eds.), *Researching Children's Experiences: Methods and Approaches* (London, UK: Sage, 2005), 1–21.

Greene, S., and Hogan, D., *Researching Children's Experiences: Methods and Methodological Issues* (London, UK: Sage, 2005).

Heath, S., Charles, V., Crow, G., and Wiles, R., 'Informed Consent, Gatekeepers and Go-betweens: Negotiating Consent in Child and Youth Orientated Institutions', *British Educational Research Journal*, 33(3) (2007), 403–417.

Hill, M., 'Ethical Considerations in Researching Children's Experiences', in S. Greene and D. Hogan (eds.), *Researching Children's Experiences: Approaches and Methods* (London: Sage, 2005), 61–86.

Holmes, R.M., *Fieldwork with Children* (Thousand Oaks, CA: Sage, 1998).

Mayall, B., 'Conversations with Children Working with Generational Issues', in P. Christensen and A. James (eds.), *Research with Children Perspectives and Practices* (London, UK and New York, NY: Falmer Press, 2000).

Pardhan, A., 'Methodological Issues and Tensions: Reflections of Conducting Ethnographic Research with Women in Booni Valley, Chitral District, Pakistan', in J. Rareiya and R. Qureshi (eds.), *Gender and Education in Pakistan* (Karachi, Pakistan: Oxford University Press, 2007), 237–256.

Pardhan, A., and Juma, A., *Gender Differences in Boys and Girls Play*, Research report (The Aga Khan University–Institute for Educational Development, Karachi, Pakistan, 2007).

Thorne, B., *Gender Play: Girls and Boys in School* (New Brunswick, NJ: Rutgers, University Press, 1993).

Vazir, N., 'Learning about Right and Wrong: Perspectives of Primary Students in a Private School in Pakistan', Ph.D. dissertation (University of Toronto, Canada, 2004).

Vazir, N., 'Researching Students' Lived Experiences: Challenges and Responses', in D.K. Behera (ed.), *Childhoods in South Asia* (New Delhi, India: Pearson Longman, 2007), 166–180.

Acknowledgement

I wish to thank the school, teachers, children, and parents for their participation in my research. I would also like to acknowledge the financial grants received from the Social Sciences and Humanities Research Council, Canada (SSHRC) and the Ontario Institute for Studies in Education, University of Toronto (OISE/UT) for funding this research. The support from my doctoral supervisor and committee members greatly facilitated the research process.

3

Obligations, Roles, and Rights
Research ethics revisited

SAIQA IMTIAZ ASIF

Introduction

Ethical issues are pervasive in research. According to Sieber (1993: 14), 'Ethics has to do with the application of moral principles to prevent harming or wronging others, to promote the good, to be respectful and to be fair'. Research in social sciences often involves dealing with people, groups and organizations. The researcher asks people questions, observes their behaviour, or collects other information about them. All of these dealings with other people raise ethical issues (Bouma, 2000). Sieber (1993) in her guide to planning ethically responsible research states that problems like deception and invasion of privacy must be given serious considerations in research planning. Sikes (2004: 25) however, is of the view that, 'Ethical considerations apply throughout the research process'. This view is supported by Mertens (1998) who believes that in the planning and implementation process of any research, ethics should be an integral part and not viewed as a burden or an afterthought. Blaxter, Hughes and Tight (1996: 149) add that 'Research ethics is about being clear about the nature of the agreement you have entered into with your research subjects or contact'. They further elaborate that ethical research involves getting the informed consent of those who are going to be interviewed, questioned or observed and from whom we take material. It also involves reaching agreements about the use, analysis and dissemination of data and its results. More important, it is about keeping such agreements when they have been reached.

It is generally held that, 'The decision to conduct research often presents a conflict between the commitment to expanding knowledge and the potential cost to the research participant' (McBurney and White, 2004: 67). Moral and ethical concerns can arise at all stages in the research process (Gregory, 2003). These phases include: research problem statement, purpose statement, research questions, data collection, data analysis and interpretation, and writing and disseminating research (Creswell, 2003).

Several associations and researchers have provided guidelines to researchers on the issue of ethics in research (e.g. BAAL;[1] BSA;[2] Creswell, 2003; Fetterman, 1998; McBurney and White, 2004; Opie, 2004; Silverman: 2000). These codes have been developed to provide guidance and establish principles to address ethical issues. Such codified principles are intended to ensure that while designing and conducting research the researchers consider all the ethical dilemmas and possible risks (Marczyk, Dematteo and Festinger, 2005). These principles are also intended to safeguard research participants from harm (Sieber and Stanley, 1988).

Such codes, however, generally fail to address divergent circumstances under which different kinds of research is conducted. Sikes (2004: 25) therefore warns that, 'on their own they may not be enough to prevent harm and hurt because the unique characteristics of such instances of research have to be considered in their own right'. Richardson draws our attention to the ethical and political dimensions of research when she asks 'How is knowledge created? By and for whom? And with what consequences for individuals, groups and society?' (1997: 102). Hence, Ezzy (2002) believes that ethical conduct of qualitative research is not confined to following guidelines provided by ethics committees. What is involved is a weighed consideration of both how data collection is conducted and how analysed data are presented. He further adds that this will vary significantly depending on the details and particularities of the situation of the research. The circumstances may differ due to the specific social, cultural and religious norms. My experience of conducting research in both rural and urban settings in Pakistan also indicates that conducting research in an ethical manner is not just a procedural matter decided by committees; rather it is, 'a political and practical matter influenced by how the researcher answers precisely these questions about the impact and consequences of the research for participants' (Ezzy, 2002: 57).

In this chapter I will discuss and illustrate with examples how ethical codes imported from the North at times cannot be applied to the divergent circumstances under which research is carried out in various research settings in countries in the South such as Pakistan. In the course of this discussion I will examine ethical dilemmas regarding researcher's and research participants' vulnerabilities encountered during my research study carried out in a rural context in Pakistan. These dilemmas highlight the mismatch of the so called 'standard universal ethical codes' with the norms of behaviour in different cultures. The chapter will also emphasize that due to culture specific realities the researchers encounter in the field, they have to modify their role in order to safeguard the rights and interest of not only the research participant but their own as well. With the help of examples from the field, I also advocate that the ethical code for researchers should recognize researchers' obligation towards the research participants thus giving them the right to modify certain codes; the reflexive nature of this exercise should, however, be shared with the wider research community for purposes of transparency and further dialogue on the issues identified by individual researchers.

Ethical dilemmas during research

In the following sections I will illustrate the complexity of ethical decision making and locate moments of such decisions within the process of my doctoral research which was essentially qualitative in nature (Asif, 2005a). Taking a reflexive stance, I will first discuss the research participants' vulnerabilities. The researcher's roles, right and obligations in the field and beyond will be discussed in subsequent sections.

Ethical dilemmas regarding research participants' vulnerabilities

In the context of research, Roberts and Roberts (1999) identify three sources from which the potential vulnerabilities of the research participants may stem, namely:

Intrinsic vulnerabilities

Personal characteristics which may limit the individual's capacities or freedoms, e.g. competence—understanding appreciation, reasoning;

Extrinsic vulnerabilities

Situational factors which may limit the individual's capacities or freedoms, e.g. anxiousness or confusion due to some particular circumstances or implicit or explicit coercion;

Relational vulnerabilities

Can occur as a result of individual's relationship with other individuals or sets of individuals, e.g. tenant/land lord, warden/prisoner, teacher/student;

These vulnerabilities are described in relation to mentally challenged people. However, these can very well be transferred to other research participants in many situations because of their peculiar circumstances such as low literacy rate or lack of awareness of basic human rights, which defined the rural setting of my research study in Pakistan. The codes of ethics for researchers do not generally recognize or give allowance for such vulnerabilities, nor do they recognize that in certain situations the research participants cannot be informed about the true intent behind the data to be collected from them.

I carried out a research study on Seraiki language in rural and urban Multan where I worked with families belonging to different income groups. Seraiki is mainly the language of a disadvantaged group inhabiting some of the poorest and most backward regions of Pakistan. The literacy rate in these regions is also the lowest in the Punjab province. In fact, most of the rural population in Seraiki regions located in Southern Punjab is illiterate. Owing to several factors, the Seraiki language is stigmatized, which, coupled with poverty, has instilled a feeling of cultural and linguistic shame amongst a large number of Seraikis (Asif, 2005b). It is because of these reasons I call my research participants vulnerable.

Intrinsic and extrinsic vulnerabilities

The guidelines generally provided for dealing with participants' consent emphasize that *Informed Consent*[3] should be sought by the researcher from the participants before starting fieldwork (McBurney and White, 2004). However, 'Gaining informed consent poses particular problems for social research' (Bouma, 2000: 197). During the course of data collection for my doctoral research, I also faced problems due to the nature of the data to be collected.

Most of the ethical guidelines suggest that information sheets should be given to the research participants, which may be written in their first language. Also, that it is necessary to obtain their signatures on the 'Informed consent form' showing their willingness to participate in the research. Such codes, however, do not take into account the differences in cultures and various settings even within one culture to which the research participants belong. In this connection, Liberman (1999: 55) observes, 'On many occasions a great portion of the ethics of our sociological practice derives from having a genuine and not merely feigned respect for the social practices that we study'.

In my particular research setting, information sheets would not have worked with illiterate or semi-literate participants. Also, I could not dare to ask for the signatures or the thumb impressions of most of my research participants because of their prior negative association with malpractices associated with signatures on forms. Hence, I explained the purpose of my research to the participants verbally; taking their signatures or thumb impressions on the 'Informed consent forms' was simply out of question as these participants would have thought that by getting them to sign a paper I was involving them in some fraud or may use their names and consent to gain some monetary benefit for myself later. Thus, I did not conform to the required standards of informed consent as defined by my institutional ethics committee. If I had done so I would have violated the norms of the community I was studying. Instead I developed and practiced an ethical code that was in conformity with the socio-cultural norms and practices of the community under study.

My general understanding of the culture of the region and an incident that I encountered at the beginning of my data collection process helped me in taking this course of action. For some data I approached a few families belonging to the low income group and requested them to participate in my research. My requirement was to record their home conversations. Three women answered that they do not talk at home; they just go about their work. My contact suggested that for the sake of recordings they may discuss anything, e.g. their problems. One of these women looked at me meaningfully and said 'hmm this way your problems will be solved but not ours' implying that by highlighting their problems on some platform I will get some monetary aid for myself in their name.

Another guideline which is provided to the researchers on the issue of informed consent is that they should 'Give information about the research to the participants...Make sure that participants understand the information given' (Ethical guidelines for Social Researchers, Faculty of Social Sciences, Lancaster University[4]), or 'Ethnographers must formally or informally seek informed consent to conduct their work (Fetterman, 1998: 138). So even when there is no compulsion for formal written consent from the participants as in the latter quotation, surely there is no escape from what 'informed' implies and necessitates. This rule also cannot be followed in its true spirit in all situations. Even though I explained the purpose of my research to the participants, that I wanted to study the language choices that people make in their home domain, I had no way of ensuring whether the participating families had fully understood the objective of my research. When I tried explaining the purpose of my research to the participants belonging to the low income group from rural areas, a question that was repeatedly asked was, 'What will you get out of working on the language of the poor people?' Similar distrust of the researcher's intentions and possible misuse of the data collected was expressed when I was interviewing a grandmother from a family in urban Multan (I also recorded the home conversations of that family). During the interview, a male member came to me and said, 'Look we don't know what your real intentions are. We just do not want to get into any kind of trouble'. In a culture where tapping the telephone, victimisation of individuals and violation of basic human rights is the order of the day, such suspicions seem justified. It was clear that these participants had consented to participate in my research only to honour the request of my friends and contacts that I had used to access them, without really understanding what it was all about (for a discussion on this issue also see chapter six).

Initially when I went to a village with my friend, she gathered some women of that village in her house and I explained to them the purpose of my research and their possible role in it as participants. When I was asking these women questions about their families to prepare their profiles to choose the ones which suited my criteria of participating families, I noticed the eagerness with which they were making sure that I write the names and ages of all their children, thinking that possibly this research will benefit them somehow in material terms. This was confirmed during my later conversations with them when they told me about the work of some NGOs working in the social and educational sector in the nearby villages. These women had heard from the inhabitants of those villages about how the women workers of those NGOs came and worked in their villages and gave them different kinds of aid. As a result, I again explained to them the scope of my research and this explanation was repeated to the two families who consented to participate in my research, to remove any misunderstanding about the purpose of my research.

Another incident that I will cite now also suggests that the ethical guidelines should be culture specific. This happened in the home of an urban family belonging to the low income group. While I was recording their home conversations, their son who was 13 at that time and studying in a *Madrassa* (seminary) walked in. He looked at me and my equipment with suspicion and started shooting questions at me about my intentions. It is pertinent to mention here that I collected my data in the winter of 2002, about 14 months after the 9/11 incident. By this time the divide between the Muslims and the rest of the world had become very deep. The fact that I was studying at a British university made me more suspicious in his eyes. As his mother had allowed me to collect data from her family he could not stop me, but during all my visits I could feel his eyes following me and noticing every single move I made and every word that I uttered. I did not encounter this reaction from his other siblings who were studying in the mainstream schools.

The instances cited above indicate that many of the participants failed to understand the objective of my research. This raises another ethical issue; although I had explained everything about my research and had obtained their verbal consent for participation, was I justified in going ahead with my research in the wake of such misplaced, 'unsaid' expectations? Can my data in this sense be called a 'legitimate datum'? The Faculty of Social Sciences, Lancaster University in its 'Ethical Guidelines for Social Researchers'[5] states that legitimate data is one 'for which consent has been obtained'. How can we say with certainty that all the participants who give their verbal and written consent to participate in the research were really 'informed', i.e. they fully understood what the research is about? Gafaranga (1998) questions the sincerity of permission granted to the researcher by the participants in carrying out the research. My point is about whether the participants really 'know' and 'understand' the objectives of the research and how the data recorded with their help would be used. These are instances of *intrinsic* and *extrinsic vulnerability* which need to be accounted for in any code of ethics. Maxey (2000) rightly states that the suitability of informed consent in a particular setting should be assessed and modified accordingly. I believe that the researchers, taking a reflexive stance, should modify the code of ethics according to the needs of the particular situation. Some restrictions however, should be imposed on these 'modifications' which I will elaborate towards the end of this chapter.

In my particular situation as mentioned above, the way I resolved this ethical dilemma was that I did not misguide the research participants. After selecting the families who were to participate in my research, I explained to them to the best of my capacity what my research was about and what cooperation I expected from them. All the 'consents' were given of their 'free will' and I also knew that my research would not have any harmful consequences for their lives as I planned to keep their names confidential.

During the course of my research, I faced another kind of dilemma. It related to whether I should give full information to some of my research participants or not. Silverman (2000: 200) states, 'both qualitative and quantitative researchers studying human subjects ponder over the dilemma of wanting to give full information to subjects but not 'contaminating' their research by informing subjects too specifically about the research question to be studied.' In keeping with the ethical guidelines laid down for researchers by my British university I gave the interviewees and some participants of my research a detailed description of the aims of my study. However, I could not possibly tell the 'matched-guise test' takers the true purpose of the test, due to the nature of the data I aimed to gather (Asif, 2005b). I used extremely general statements about how I would use the responses of the participants. The nature of this test is such that had I told the respondents what I wanted to achieve out of this test it would have invalidated the data. For such situations harmless 'white lies' which assist in collecting valid and reliable data have been allowed by the experts (Burgess, 1984: 201). Sikes (2000: 25) recommends, 'A useful acid test when considering methodologies and procedures is to ask yourself how you would personally feel if you or your children or your friends were 'researched' by means of them'. In this case I did not have any qualms whatsoever about the use of this technique; therefore, I went ahead with it.

Relational vulnerabilities

Another noteworthy issue in the context of my research in a rural setting in Pakistan is whether participants felt pressurized to give their consent or were these given with their 'free will'. But a question that arose for me was, 'How 'free' is free will?' Lipson (1994) questions the ethics of using such socially produced consent. Some of the rural families participating in my research were approached through their landlord's wife who invited the women living on her farm to her house and told me to talk to them and 'choose' whichever families 'suited me' as my research participants. In such circumstances could the families I chose say no to their landlord's wife and refuse to participate in my research? This kind of situation was not just confined to the rural setting. In the city I encountered a more or less similar situation. The schoolteachers who I interviewed were approached through their school heads following the proper decorum. In both type of schools, state-run primary schools and elite English medium schools, the principals called the teachers and pointing towards me informed them that I wanted to interview them. They were not asked whether they wanted to be interviewed; rather they were just told. This could be due to the hierarchical culture in Pakistani schools and the society at large. However, I believe that this may happen in any situation where people are not aware of their rights as research participants (also see chapter six in this volume).

The question that arises here is that when employees are 'told' by their employer or boss that they are to be interviewed by a researcher, can these employees refuse? Do the employees not feel pressurized into giving their consent? As mentioned earlier, such instances can happen anywhere and in any kind of research. The Nuremberg Code, however, states 'The voluntary consent of the human subject is absolutely essential' (cited in Marczyk, Dematteo and Festinger, 2005: 236). I feel that such guidelines fail to take into account the power relations in different research settings.

In the light of different kinds of vulnerabilities discussed above, I will now discuss, in the next section, the need to consider a revised role of the researcher in the field. I believe that the researcher has an obligation to safeguard the rights of the research participants. However, this obligation also entitles the researcher to use his/her right to assess the situation regarding the research ethics and take decisions appropriate to the socio-cultural 'norms' of the research participants and the setting in which the research is located. These 'decisions' which may often be incongruent with the standard research ethics guidelines are necessary to conduct valid research (see chapter one).

Roles, Rights, and Obligations

As illustrated in the previous sections, every research situation is novel due to social, cultural, economic, political and religious factors. The researcher has to assume different roles in different settings due to the specific demands of that particular situation (see also chapter two).

In my particular research setting my image in the field was that of an educated, urban, upper-middle class Muslim Multani woman. With all these attributes there was a well-defined role model, with a high positive value, available to me. I was expected to conform to this model and in this very conformity lay my acceptance as a researcher both in rural and urban Multan, something which I needed from the participating families and the interviewees. Living up to this image was not very difficult for me as I was a part of that culture and was well aware of its demands and specifications.

In the previous section I have discussed the relational vulnerabilities with reference to the research participants. Here I will demonstrate that the role(s) that researchers assume in the field also make them vulnerable in several ways which can affect the nature and amount of data collected in the field. For example, a major limitation in my research is that compared to females there is less data from male participants. Coming from the same culture I had already anticipated that there would be less adult male participation in conversations in the home domain. In Multani culture women and men who are not closely related to each other do not interact freely, even in the home environment. I knew that during my presence in the homes of the participating families, men would avoid coming to the room where I would be. This is their way of giving respect to their female family guests. I also knew that if I would insist on male participation then, firstly, there would be some raised eyebrows about my 'modesty' which might result in their mistrust in me; secondly, the conversation in the room would not be natural as men would be self-conscious in my presence and it would also affect the interaction of the other family members. Hence, I had to modify my role from an objective researcher to that of a 'Multani researcher' who was familiar with the local cultural norms and was therefore expected to understand and respect the right of the research participants to behave in whatever way they were comfortable with. This obligation towards my research participants forced me, in turn, to modify my research plans. Brewer (2000: 84) rightly remarks, 'the ethnographer's behaviour must cement relationships with the people whose natural environment it is'. In three homes men came and joined us in the room but their position in relation to me was different and 'safe'. One was my relative's family who were also very good friends; it was therefore natural for the father of that family to join us during my conversations with the female participants in their home. One of the sons of the second family had been my student in the university so he, unlike his elder brother, felt comfortable in coming and talking to me on different occasions during the time I spent with that family. The grandfather of the third family also came and spent some time with us in his home. This was by virtue of his age which gave him the status to call me his daughter. My intention in the study was to observe and record naturally occurring speech in the home domain. For this I did not want to stage an artificial scene. Nor did I want to compromise the quality of the data by conducting the whole of the research amongst my relatives or close friends to ensure sufficient male participation. As a result, there was lesser participation by adult males in home conversations but I knew that this was a real reflection of the family life in Multan. Thus I exercised my right as a researcher to tackle this situation in a way which allowed me to fulfill my obligation not only towards my research participants but also to my research by obtaining 'uncontaminated' data. In the light of this experience I strongly believe that if the researchers' *roles* deviate from the general behaviour recommended for them, it should be the *right* of the researcher to assume different roles in order to safeguard the rights of the research participants. This will help them fulfil their *obligation* to the research participants and to the research itself.

Fieldwork, like all other experiences, is an embodied one and this embodiment has consequences for our research. Relationships in the field apart from behaviour also depend on monitoring and perhaps modification of the non-verbal messages communicated, for example, by the researcher's body language and dress code (Warren and Hackney: 2000). In the field I had to keep up with the norms of external propriety in the host culture. Following the observation by Ganesh (1993) that 'A woman with a traditional profile puts people at ease' (p. 136), I wore a big '*chaddar*' (a piece of cloth wrapped around the body) and covered my face when stepping outside the homes in the village. Also, following the practice of the women of the families I visited, I kept my head covered even while only women and children were present in the house. This was my way of showing respect for the local norms; I felt this was also my obligation towards the local people and my contact person who had made my entry in the field possible.

It is rightly argued that 'sensitivity to the appropriate protocol can enhance the interviewer's effectiveness' (Fetterman, 1998: 44). I never sat alone in the room to interview the male participants. While interviewing the village school head I kept my eyes downcast just as he had his gaze low most of the time even while we were talking to each other. Considering how important eye contact is in communication in the Western world, I can understand how some readers might wonder how this can be described as successful communication. I remember the frustration of an American colleague teaching in my University when at times her male students would keep their gaze low while talking to her. She always felt that they were hiding something from her or were being dishonest to her. It was neither. In conservative setups in Pakistan when the members of the opposite sex who are 'na mehrum' (with whom one is allowed by religion to marry) communicate, they are to lower their gaze. This is in keeping with the teachings of Islam. In cases where power relations are involved then sometimes during communication, even amongst the members of the same sex, the person in the subordinate position keeps his/her gaze low as a mark of respect. This is a social norm. In the city neither my interviewees nor I follow this practice. However, I had to do so in the village as the changed situation demanded that I modify my behaviour patterns according to the role assigned to me of an esteemed guest (in the village, I was known as the landlord's guest; some research participants also considered me his wife's relative). Hence, I felt obliged to follow the norms practiced by the women of the landlord's family. Also, it was my obligation towards my friend's family to live up to the local image of a 'modest' woman. Not doing so would have jeopardized my reputation in the village; also, it might have had negative repercussions for my relationship with my friend. More importantly, it would have created a general mistrust for the overall community of researchers. In this sense I also felt that I had an obligation to the future generations of researchers working in similar settings in Pakistan.

The difference in my gender and that of my interviewee also played a role in selecting the location for these interviews. For example, I wanted to observe the school environment and interview the school head in his school. However, my friend's husband considered it best to invite him to their home for the interview as the people in the village would not have approved of my going there for this purpose. As a woman from the landlord's 'family' was going to meet with (interview) the male school head, he was invited to the women's quarters but made to sit in the open courtyard where the interview was conducted. According to local cultural norms, it is not appropriate for a strange man to enter any of the rooms in the women's quarters. In addition, my friend's husband 'chaperoned' me throughout the interview. Being a part of Multani culture I knew that this was his way of extending the same respect to me which he would have accorded to his sister, wife or daughter. He exercised his right to follow his normal behaviour which I felt obliged to follow.

I want to make one thing clear here; there was no external pressure on me to conform to the local norms nor did this limit my findings because being a part of the local Multani culture I fully understood and respected the social norms. In fact, in my everyday life I also conform to some of these socio-cultural norms while deviating from others. However, during my research, I felt that conformity would help me negotiate my role as an 'insider-outsider' which, in turn, would help win the trust of my research participants. Phillips (2000) rightly observes that during the research process in the field we have to play up or play down aspects of our identity to maintain the flow of good quality information. However, a note of caution is required here. While I strongly believe that it is the right of the researchers to exercise their own judgment for assuming certain role(s) in the field, it should be their obligation to protect the interests of the research participants and contacts that allowed them access to the research site/participants in the first place. The central role of reflexivity in this interplay of roles, rights and obligations cannot be emphasized enough for qualitative researchers, particularly in taking decisions that may seem to conflict with the 'standard' code of ethics.

Revisiting Research Ethics

No set of ethical standards can possibly anticipate every ethical dilemma a researcher is likely to face in the field and even at the later stages of dissemination of findings. As demonstrated in the above discussion, many a times, neatly laid down rules developed in and 'imported' from the North cannot possibly be followed in international research in specific socio-cultural settings in the South. As mentioned by several other contributors to this collection (for example, see chapter four) the reality of the writers of the guidebooks about research practices may sometimes be quite different from the reality of the researchers and the context in which the research is being conducted. Thus, in many situations the code of ethics has to be adapted or even relinquished when the researcher comes face to face with various kinds of reality in the field. It is therefore essential that ethics committees of local universities and research organizations in the South must devise local ethical standards and principles. Furthermore, every effort should be made to sensitize the researchers towards the application of these codes because it is the researcher's obligation to protect and safeguard the rights of the participants.

We cannot, however, neglect the presence of sub-cultures within the local culture so the researchers should also be encouraged to use their judgment and modify or even abandon certain codes in certain situations for ensuring the validity of their findings. This, however, raises a few questions: how can one ensure that the researchers' assessment of specific situations is sound and their decisions ethical and, therefore, acceptable both to institutional ethics committees in the North and the research community at large? I believe that these issues can be resolved by the local researchers using reflexivity to capitalize on their local knowledge as also their knowledge and understanding the need for ethical research in the light of international guidelines for research.

Conclusion and Recommendations

Researchers do not work in a vacuum; rather they participate in the lives of other human beings which puts a responsibility on them to follow a code of ethics that respects their informants (Fetterman, 1998). 'Researchers who do not review ethical problems carefully are negligent toward society' (McBurney and White, 2004: 52). The credibility of research is not built just on originality in research or using and acknowledging the right sources but also on the maintenance of the highest ethical standards. The researchers should thus be made aware of and be sensitized towards these issues.

Since there is no universally applicable code of ethics, keeping in view the local realities, the local research organizations and universities should devise their own code of ethics. A few developing countries like India, Uganda and South Africa have already formulated their own national ethical codes which provide an intermediate step between the international code of ethics for research and decisions about how these should be applied on a country-by-country basis.[6] In Pakistan there exists a dire need to devise local ethical standards and principles and sensitize the researchers towards the application of these codes because, 'Without adequate training and supervision, the neophyte researcher can unwittingly become an unguarded projectile bringing turbulence to the field, fostering personal trauma (for researcher and researched), and even causing damage to the discipline' (Punch, 1994: 93). Finally, it will fall upon the researchers to choose what is best in the interest of their participants and their research without compromising their humanity or their research data. Gregory (2003: 28–29) rightly advises that 'Human beings, their interests and concerns, lie at the very heart of the researcher. Given that it is human beings who are to be exposed to the research endeavour, we do well to remain sensitive to the morally laden nature of our dealings with one another.'

Notes

1. <www.baal.org.uk/goodprac.htm>, retrieved 12 December 2006
2. <www.britsoc.org.uk/ethgu2.htm>, retrieved 10 December 2006
3. Informed consent means, 'prospective research participants must be fully informed about the procedures and risks involved and must give their consent to participate', <www.socialresearchmethods.net/kb/ethics.htm>, retrieved 12 December 2006
4. <www.lancs.ac.uk/fss/resources/ethics/guidelines.htm>, retrieved 12 December 2006
5. <www.lancs.ac.uk/fss/resources/ethics/guidelines.htm>, retrieved 12 December 2006
6. <www.scidev.net/dossiers/index.cfm?fuseaction=dossierfulltext&Dossier=5>, retrieved 12 December 2006

References

Asif, S.I., 'Siraiki: A Sociolinguistic Study of Language Desertion', Ph.D. thesis (Lancaster University, UK, 2005a).

Asif, S.I., 'Shame: A Major Cause of Language Desertion', *Journal of Research* (Faculty of Language & Islamic Studies, BZU), 8 (2005b), 1–13.

Asif, S.I., 'Attitudes towards Siraiki Language', *Journal of Research* (Humanities, BZU), 15 (2005c), 11–27.

Blaxter, L., Hughes, C., and Tight, M., *How to Research* (Buckingham: Open University Press, 1996).

Bouma, G.D., *The Research Process*, 4e (Victoria: Oxford University Press, 2000).

Brewer, J.D., *Ethnography* (Buckingham Philadelphia: Open University Press, 2000).

Burgess, R.G., *In the Field: An Introduction to Field Research* (London: Allen and Unwin, 1984).

Creswell, J.W., *Research Design: Qualitative, Quantitative, and Mixed Methods Approaches*, 2e (London: Thousand Oaks; New Delhi: Sage Publications, 2003).

Ezzy, D., *Qualitative Analysis: Practice and Innovation* (London: Routledge, 2002).

Fetterman, D.M., *Ethnography: Step by Step* (Thousand Oaks, CA: Sage, 1998).

Gafaranga, J., 'Elements of Order in Bilingual Talk: Kinyarwanda-French Language Alternation', Ph.D. thesis (Lancaster University, UK, 1998).

Ganesh, K., 'Breaching the Wall of Difference: Fieldwork and a Personal Journey to Srivaikuntam, Tamilnadu', in D. Bell, P. Caplan, and W. J. Karim, (eds.) *Gendered Fields: Women, Men and Ethnography* (London: Routledge, 1993), 128–42.

Gregory, I., *Ethics in Research* (London; New York: Continuum, 2003).

Liberman, K., 'From Walkabout to Meditation: Craft and Ethics in Field Enquiry', *Qualitative Inquiry*, 5 (1) (1999), 47–63.

Lipson, J.G., 'Ethical Issues in Ethnography', in Morse, J. M., (ed.), *Critical Issues in Qualitative Research Methods* (Thousand Oaks, CA: Sage, 1994), 333–55.

Marczyk, G., DeMatto D., and Festinger, D., *Essentials of Research Design and Methodology* (New Jersey: John Wiley & Sons Inc, 2005).

Maxey, I., 'Informed Consent and the Conspiracy of Silence: Some Ethical and Practical Problems Raised by Fieldwork', *Swansea Geographer*, 35 (2000), 57–70.

McBurney, D.H., and White, T.L., *Research Methods*, 6e (Belmont: Wadsworth, 2004).

Mertens, D.M., *Research Methods in Education and Psychology: Integrating Diversity with Quantitative and Qualitative Approaches* (London: Thousand Oaks; New Delhi: Sage Publications, 1998).

Phillips, M., 'Theories of Positionality and Ethnography in Researching the Rural', in A. Hughes, C. Morris, and S. Seymour (eds.), *Ethnography and Rural Research* (Cheltenham: Countryside Community Press, 2000), 28–51.

Punch, M., 'Politics and Ethics in Qualitative Research', in N. Denzin, and Y. Lincoln (eds.), *The Handbook of Qualitative Research*, 2e (Thousand Oaks, CA: Sage, 1994).

Richardson, L., *Fields of Play: Constructing an Academic Life* (New Brunswick, Rutgers University Press, 1997).

Roberts, L., and Roberts, B., 'Psychiatric Research Ethics: An Overview of Evolving Guidelines and Current Ethical Dilemmas in the Study of Mental Illness', *Biological Psychiatry*, 46: 1025–38.

Sieber, J., 'The Ethics and Politics of Sensitive Research', in C. Renzetti, C. Lee, and R. Lee (eds.), *Researching Sensitive Topics* (London: Sage, 1993).

Sieber, J., and Stanley, B., 'Ethical and Professional Dimensions of Socially Sensitive Research', *American Psychologist*, 42 (1988) 49–55.

Sikes, P., 'Methodology, Procedures and Ethical Concerns', in C. Opie (ed.), *Doing Educational Research: A Guide for First Time Researchers* (New Delhi: Vistaar Publications, 2004), 15–33.

Silverman, D., *Doing Qualitative Research: A Practical Handbook* (London: Thousand Oaks; New Delhi: Sage Publications, 2000).

Warren, C.A.B., and Hackney, J.K., *Gender Issues in Ethnography*, 2e Sage University Papers series on Qualitative Research Methods, Vol. 9 (Thousand Oaks, CA: Sage, 2000).

4

Ethical standards and ethical environment

Tensions and a way forward[1]

RASHIDA QURESHI[2]

The ten-point Nuremberg Code provided the guiding principles for conducting 'ethically' sound research involving human beings in the post Second World War era. These principles have been incorporated into the codes of research by different disciplines and their associations; for example, Australian Association of Mathematics Teachers, British Sociological Association, Canadian Psychological Association and many other associations/societies. In most western countries formally designated groups monitor the 'standards' of ethics in research, for instance, Institutional Review Boards (IRB) in the US are responsible for approving and reviewing all research projects involving human subjects especially in medical and behavioral sciences.

In Pakistan, no formal arrangements at institutional levels exist to approve, monitor, and review research projects that are undertaken in various fields.[3] The discipline specific professional associations in Pakistan usually depend on the codes of ethics in research which are borrowed from the West along with research text books for these disciplines. The ethical standards provided by the North, however, do not take into consideration what Blackburn (2001) terms as the 'ethical environment' of non-Western contexts. By ignoring the latter, the codes of ethics developed in the North disregard what is distinct about a local culture despite the fact that the uniqueness of each culture shapes and is reflected in the individual experiences in developing country contexts such as Pakistan which; '...could be used more to enrich the texts that guide us on how to do research. This is where experience mediates the rules rather than the other way round. The only way we can truly come up with effective codes and guidelines is if experience is used directly to inform them' (Makkar, 2002: 81). Researchers from developing countries are constantly faced with ethical dilemmas arising out of the interplay between *rules* which are referred to as ethical standards in this chapter and *norms* which following Blackburn (2001), I would refer to as ethical environment in a socio-cultural setting. These tensions and struggles that shape researchers' experiences underpin this chapter.

The chapter is divided into two sections: Part I highlights the ethical dilemmas that are born out of a tension between ethical standards and ethical environment. These predicaments are discussed with reference to: the research participants, research outcomes and researcher. In order to make my argument, I will mainly draw upon my personal experience of being a community development researcher and thesis supervisor of graduate students' research in education. The third source is the experiences of my colleagues and students elicited through formal and informal conversations and focus group discussions. For the ethical standards of research I refer to the American Educational Research Association (AERA) and the British Educational Research Association (BERA) which are mostly referred to by my students, my colleagues and most of the researchers I meet in Pakistan in the field of education. Although my examples are contextually situated in the ethical environment of Pakistan, their theoretical applications are relevant to similar settings in other parts of the world. Part II is based on finding ways to mediate the tensions between ethical standards and ethical environment without compromising the integrity of the researchers and the quality of research studies.

Before moving to Part I of this chapter, I will first elaborate the two terms—'ethical environment' and 'ethical standards' as used in this chapter.

Ethical environment and ethical standards

Every society has its own sets of ideas which are rooted in that particular context. Local knowledge, local culture and traditions form a holistic circle that governs every aspect of local life. Hence, any research that explores an aspect of local life, whether it is economic, social, political, environmental and/or psychological will have to be directed by the set of norms developed, agreed upon and 'approved' by local communities/people because these contextual norms direct their behaviour. This normative structure of a particular context is what Blackburn (2001) refers to as 'ethical environment':

> ...the surrounding climate of ideas about how to live. It [ethical environment] determines what we find acceptable or unacceptable, admirable or contemptible. It determines our conception of when things are going well and when they are going badly. It determines our conception of what is due to us, and what is due from us, as we relate to others. It shapes our emotional responses, determining what is a cause of pride or shame, or anger or gratitude, or what can be forgiven and what cannot. It gives us our standards-our standards of behaviour (p. 1).

These 'standards' (with a small 's') dictate what is ethical or otherwise in a particular setting at a particular moment. Hence the ethical environment reflects contextual realities that govern every aspect of formal and informal relationships in time and space. In contrast, the formal ethical standards are professional codes that govern a specific relationship in time and space. The following vignette reflects an interaction between the two.

> From her conversation I had a sense that she felt acutely disappointed at the thought of not being named in the thesis. She raised a number of questions...I tried to make Amina Karim see the risks that the

research participants take...In the end she agreed with me implying through her words that if these are the rules regarding the research ethics then I suppose you have to follow them. (Halai, 2001: 281–282)

The 'rules' being referred to in the above conversation, were the ethical standards of the British Educational Research Association (BERA) for conducting educational research. The research context was a Pakistani school and caught between the two was a Pakistani doctoral student at the University of Oxford. Halai, like her fellow educational researchers in the developing countries, was constantly struggling to strike a balance between the standards stipulated by BERA and the local norms and folkways practiced in Pakistan. She was expected to follow the ethical guidelines based on the professional codes of conduct developed in the North that required her to protect the confidentiality of her respondent by making her anonymous. This was in conflict with the moral codes of conduct embedded in the local culture and practices which called for publicly acknowledging the 'good' work done by her respondent. In this environment the use of pseudonym purported to a lie in order to cheat the respondent out of her due share of 'prestige' (op. cit., p. 282). Halai's respondent had been working with her for quite some time now. Most of her colleagues as well as friends and relatives knew of her as being one of the research participants. What would their reaction be when they did not see not 'her' name in the final report? The professional integrity of a researcher would be at stake if local people perceived of him/her as a liar or cheater. Thus by following international standards, it is possible that the professional reputation of a particular researcher may be damaged; more important, the possibilities for future research in this setting could also be jeopardized.

Similarly one of my graduate students was conducting research on classroom practices of particular subject teachers. The student completed her interviews, transcribed these and took them back to her research participants for member check. In the meantime, she had also completed her first level of analysis by identifying important categories and themes for the second round. One of her research participants disowned some of her earlier statements for fear of being recognized by the head despite the promises of anonymity and confidentiality. Ethically the student-researcher was bound to delete the information she had gathered and as a result lost a very important theme in her analysis which limited the scope of her study (Focus group discussion). In contrast, for the research participants in Halai's study (2001), as mentioned above, the idea of being anonymous was not beneficial as 'neither teacher was happy with the idea of pseudonyms and measures taken to ensure confidentiality and anonymity' (p. 281) which are amongst the basic principles prescribed by the professional ethical standards of research. The issues associated with implementing ethical principles encoded in formal Codes of Conduct/ethical standards of research as they relate to research participants, research outcomes and the researcher are discussed in the following section.

Part I: Ethical dilemmas

Related to research participants

One of the principles of professional ethical standards is that participants should be given a reasonable explanation of the purpose and procedures of research and 'honesty should characterize the relationship between researchers and participants' (Strike, Anderson, Curren, Geel, Pritchard and Robertson, 2002:44). In Pakistan, with a majority of people being illiterate and research culture being weak, the meaning of research itself is hard to explain. Pardhan (2007) while conducting research for her Master's thesis in Booni valley of Chitral, Pakistan, told her research participants that she was writing a book about their life experiences because her participants did not understand what research was and what writing a thesis meant. I faced a similar situation in my own interaction with different groups of rural women from the North West Frontier Province (NWFP)[4], Pakistan, when I was collecting data on female education

(Qureshi, 2006). The women I interviewed were wondering why the 'educated' world would be interested in their viewpoints ('what can you possibly learn from us', 'we have never set foot into the western style formal schools'). Hence, I had to give various reasons to my research participants in order to gain entry, such as: I was writing their story for a local newspaper; I was writing a book, or collecting information for a government project. These terms seemed to be easier for them to understand and in most cases they accepted these as the purpose of my visits. But were these really the purpose of my research? How could I explain to these women that I was really interested in understanding how the manipulated interpretation of religion during the British colonial rule had condemned both men and women to the state of illiteracy (Qureshi, 2006). Was I deceiving them because '…we all know by experience that providing partial information can be as misleading as withholding information' (Eisner, 1998:217). But do the above accounts of the purpose of research even qualify as 'partial information?' When I raised this as an issue of 'deception' with my colleagues and graduate students, the consensus was that research participants were usually told 'half truths' but none was willing to consider it as 'deception.' Instead, a unanimous response was that according to Western standards it may be 'deception' but in the Pakistani context, where we are still far from developing a contextually relevant and shared understanding of the meanings of research amongst the social researchers and the research participants, it is 'not deception but just the right kind of information for participant (s) to understand the purpose of our activities if not the purpose of our research' (Focus group discussion).

In addition to the difficulties and major ethical dilemmas involved in sharing the purpose and procedures of research, ethical standards and the ethical environment in Pakistan also diverge on the issues of informed consent, voluntary consent and voluntary withdrawal. Given the above state of affairs where research participants are furnished with what some may define as half truths, how informed would they be to make an informed decision, let alone an informed choice? Furthermore, informed and voluntary consent is an individual concern in the North. Both the American Educational Research Association (AERA) and the British Educational Research Association (BERA) guidelines recommend seeking informed consent from *individual, adult research participants*. In contrast, in Pakistan for example, for one of my life history projects in the rural areas, a local woman (in her late thirties) shared a story of her personal transformation from a disinterested community member to a devoted social activist. With her permission (asked and given openly amongst a group of friends) the story was written for an organizational newsletter. Since she insisted on being recognized for her contribution, her real name and the real context was used. The very next day I was confronted by a group of her close and angry relatives because I had not 'sought' their permission before publishing such a 'defaming' article about a member of their clan. The consent of an individual, in general, and of a woman, in particular, did not count much, as according to them the matter involved the honour of the whole clan. It is needless to say that the organization in question had to withdraw that particular issue of the newsletter. Moreover, due to the wrath of the local people, the life history research project was also abandoned.

Another incident of research in a similar setting involved the so called 'voluntary participation' and 'voluntary withdrawal' of the research participants. I was part of a research team where rural mothers of primary school age girls in a remote area of North West Frontier Province (NWFP) were the research participants. Despite the fact that the research team interviewing women was all-female, village elders did not allow the research participants to be contacted directly. Male researchers who were also part of the research team were asked to explain the purpose of research to a Jirga[5]. The Jirga was especially interested in knowing the 'kind' of information to be elicited from women. Once satisfied, the village elders allowed the female team to proceed. Yet, in almost every house, I noticed the presence of at least one man listening to the exchange between female researchers and their participants (later we learnt that these men kept the Jirga updated). On every alternate day, one of our male researcher had to present to the Jirga a 'progress report' about the information exchange especially between female researchers and the local participants which could be considered a kind of member check; as gatekeepers, the authorities were keeping a check on the kind of information shared with 'outsiders.' Despite conforming to the ethical environment and the fact that the women had talked to the researchers with the Jirga's permission, the research team had to leave its work incomplete in some villages as one of the Jirga elders did not approve of the exchange of information between researchers and women participants of that particular community. In such an ethical environment, the notions of consent and withdrawal have implications on the quality of research in contexts like Pakistan, which are different from those embodied in international ethical standards. For instance, the Jirga, acting as a gatekeeper gave its 'consent' to researchers to gather information as long as the information, according to the members of the Jirga, was '...acceptable... admirable,...cause of pride...' (Blackburn, 2001:1). What if the 'withdrawal' coincides with unearthing of information that truly reflects the phenomenon under study but the gatekeepers perceive that 'things...are going badly' (ibid). The doubts about the authenticity and threats to the credibility and dependability of such information will cast a shadow on the professional reputation of researchers working in such an environment. This suggests that the very definition of a 'participant' also needs to be revisited in a context like Pakistan, where in order to reach the intended research participants, one needs to get permission from 'gatekeepers' who not only monitor what information is being given but also have the authority to censor that information. In contexts like these, we need to ask who the actual research participant is—the person who is directly engaged in a collaborative process of generating knowledge or those whose stamp of approval is required to collect and use information for research purposes. Moreover, this leads to an ethical dilemma for the researcher: whose version of 'reality' shall s/he report, the actual participants or the gatekeepers[6]? All these questions acquire a specific significance because they relate directly to the credibility and 'truth value' of knowledge generated in specific local contexts.

As stated earlier, the literacy rate in Pakistan is very low; hence, obtaining 'written' informed consent, a requirement internationally for ethical research purposes, is another contentious issue in relation to local realities. According to the 'Economic Survey of Pakistan 2004–05' only half of the country's population is literate. Among female population, 40 out of 100 and among males, 65 per cent can read and write; in rural areas, the percentages are lower—29 per cent of females and 58 per cent of males. In such a context, getting written consent is not only problematic but can also be a source of conflict between the researcher and 'influential others'. One of my graduate students faced a situation where his research participant, although a literate person, was reluctant to put his signature on a piece of paper claiming that his promise (his verbal consent to be a participant) should carry more weight than a 'miserable' signature on a 'worthless piece of paper' (shared in focus group discussion). It is important to note that in the ethical environment of Pakistan in general, and in the rural areas in particular, where this participant came from, a verbal promise or word of mouth is associated with personal honour and integrity of the speaker. Although given informally, the verbal consent carries more weight especially amongst friends, than written consent or agreement. In fact, anyone who seeks one's signature is often suspected as it is feared that s/he may use it in a legal battle later to incriminate them. Since the social identity that was being bestowed upon the student-researcher by his research participant was 'friend of a friend' (Shamim, 1993), the expectation was that the student researcher would not insist on obtaining consent in writing (see Asif in this book and Pardhan, 2007 for further discussion of this point). In the same vein, one can also question the utility of consent, whether verbal or written on two accounts.

First, getting consent from participants entails more than 'getting permission' in the formal sense of the word. Researchers not only need permission to gain entry into the field but they also need to sustain it by building trusting relations with their collaborators making 'consent', 'participation' and 'withdrawal' not one time gestures but part of an ongoing negotiation/re-negotiation process directed more by the ethical environmental standards than the professional ethical standards of research.

Second, what if the participants sign the informed consent form without even realizing the significance of this act? Halai (2001) provides a snapshot of a situation where, 'It appeared that my initial conversation with them [the research participants], undertaken at the outset of the research, had not been very helpful in enabling them to see what they had agreed to when they signed the consent form' (Halai, 2001:283). Similar examples were also reported by a number of my supervisees, who were working with teachers whose participation was secured through 'gatekeepers'; these teachers were nominated by their school heads to work as research participants which affected the quality of data collected (also see Rareiya in this book). The participants were well aware that withdrawal from the research study for which they had been nominated might harm their relationship with the school head. Hence, for such participants, the signing of an informed consent was not a voluntary act. In fact, for many it was not more than a mere 'formality'.

Yet another ethical dilemma for the qualitative researchers is the notion of 'justice' as it relates to who gets included/excluded from the study sample. One of our graduate students reported that a group of angry parents confronted her during her study and demanded to know why their children were not being included in her study particularly if it was going to be beneficial for students (shared in focus group discussion). Their 'notion' of justice did not match with the professional views of justice which the researcher was trying to apply. It seemed the parents' major concern was: how the 'exclusion' of their children from the study may affect the self-esteem and motivation levels of their children.

However, the researcher was clearly looking at the phenomenon of inclusion/exclusion in relation to her training in research and research ethics directed by the professional codes of conduct (see also Pardhan in this book).

Related to the notion of justice are the notions of 'risk' and 'harm' which a graduate student (and, by implication, the community of researchers) learnt the hard way. This particular student was conducting his research in an all girls' schools in Karachi. He had obtained the permission of the head teacher, teachers and parents before starting his research as required by the ethical standards of conducting research. He never asked the research participants to stay behind after school which may put them at risk by having to go home alone. Little did he anticipate that the classification of 'harm', situated within the local norms, was defined differently in the ethical environment of a highly gendered society from the ethical standards developed elsewhere (Khan, 2008). His research was in progress when two of his research participants, who were sisters, decided to drop out of the study because their visiting uncle had told off their father for letting his girls interact with a male stranger. The girls were afraid that if they continued to take part in his research, they would be stopped from attending school (shared in focus group discussion). The student was not prepared for this kind of harm a *male* researcher could do to his female research participants; it was not mentioned in the global ethical standards he had used to guide his research. This indicates that in a context such as Pakistan, risk and harm are defined by cultural codes and a researcher will have to negotiate and re-negotiate with his/her collaborators to define and re-define what constitutes risk or what is meant by harm in that particular ethical environment. It is also important to recognize that the definitions of risk and harm are not only situational but are also evolutionary. They are shaped and re-shaped as the research activity progresses and, therefore, require constant negotiation by the researcher within specific research settings.

Related to research outcome

Ethical standards in research also apply to research outcomes including data ownership, intellectual property and publication. These need to be included in any discussion related to ethical environment. The professional codes governing the rights to intellectual property are the product of a technical process with legalistic orientations where authorship and ownership has to be determined individually even when it is the team that is being acknowledged. In contrast, cultural codes are the product of socially constructed processes with multiple collaborators from all walks of life each contributing toward collective wisdom. This gives rise to ethical dilemmas that social scientists have to grapple with especially when the source of knowledge is oral histories. For example, intellectual property rights acquire a very different dimension in stable rural communities, in particular, where common knowledge, shared values and common understanding are cherished and all knowledge is public property. In such an ethical environment an individual statement would embody shared knowledge and folk wisdom which cannot be attributed solely to one individual or even a small group of individuals. For instance, I was talking to a group of teachers about the qualities of a good teacher (work in progress). Majority of them said that 'teacher is like a candle. S/he consumes him/her but gives lights to others.' Although the quote was the same, the source was not; 'I heard my parents say that...', or 'my Grandma used to say that...' or 'our elders told us...'. I heard the same quote from a mother whose 'elders' told her that mothers were like candles. So who should this quote be ascribed to? Similarly, there are folk stories which have been handed down from generation to generation with each generation adding some new detail. What reference or citation will a researcher give? These folk stories, folk songs, local proverbs etc., are common property—so what guidelines for intellectual property would a researcher follow?

Tied to the issue of intellectual property rights is the right to be recognized as a researcher. The social scientists of the South, including Pakistan, are engaged in producing new knowledge despite all the ethical dilemmas and subsequent challenges mentioned above. However, in order to be recognized by 'experts', this knowledge has to be published and disseminated widely. Given the weak local reading culture in general, and research culture in particular, the number of academic journals in Pakistan is limited. Besides, 'publishing in international journals is more prestigious because it is perceived to be expert knowledge which is more privileged and thus ranks higher compared to local publications' (Focus group discussion). However, the knowledge that is to be published in the North requires adherence to the ethical guidelines of the West based on western values and norms[7]. The paradoxical situation for the social scientists from the South is that if they follow the global guidelines, their work may reflect an alienated version of the local reality and thus undermine their integrity locally. On the other hand, if they take into consideration the local realities, they may be penalized for being too parochial and not following the internationally agreed principles of ethical research practices. This may result in under representation of the social scientists from the South in an academic community mainly dominated by the North.

Related to researcher

In the professional codes of research ethics, heavy emphasis is placed on issues related to consent. Hence researchers tend to look at these issues only from the perspective of the research participants (Corrigan, 2003; Roberts, 2002; Roberts and Roberts, 1999). In a developing country context like Pakistan, where the cultural codes governing human interactions are relational, the ethical environmental standards bind researchers in many ways. For instance, the range of choices and the degrees of freedom available to a researcher are determined by how s/he is introduced to community members and what relational category/categories are assigned to him/her. This is analogous to what Roberts and Roberts (1999) have identified as 'relational vulnerability.' Although researchers are concerned about how relations with other individuals or sets of individuals make a research participant vulnerable, I contend that in contexts like Pakistan, researchers too experience relational vulnerability. For example, in one of my research projects (work in progress), I was interviewing a teacher at her place in a semi-urban setting. As I was talking to her about her right to terminate the interview anytime she wished to, I could see the shock on her face:

> That would be a sin because you are not only elder to me [reference was to biological age and by implication life experiences] but also our guest. It would also be rude of me because you have come so far especially for this...I am not a scholar but you are.... You know better what to ask so why should I decline to offer information.

As she was creating multiple identities for me, not only was she spelling out her own duties in relation to each of these, she was also setting boundaries for me. In that ethical environment, I was an elder to whom deference should be accorded. I was also a guest who should not be refused anything. Moreover, I was also an expert whose authority and power was being recognized by the research participant. Most important, I was a woman, a 'buddy.' My obligation was to behave in a 'befitting' manner which entailed respecting their culture and not asking inappropriate questions that would hurt or offend my younger hostess. Since I, as a researcher, did not surface anywhere in the host of identities assigned to me in that ethical environment, my identity as a researcher became vulnerable and contingent upon meeting the obligations of my expected multiple 'relations.'

My relational vulnerability became even more pronounced when my hostess introduced me to other participants as 'friend of a friend' (Shamim, 1993). This resonates with what Pardhan (2007) experienced while collecting data; '...I realized that I would not be free to choose the research participants for my study...Zarina's networks became mine...because of my gender and the culture I was in. I had no choice' (p. 245). To me it was very clear that the relationship between me and my research participants was being defined by a moral reference where reputation of the referent plays a major role in determining whether a researcher will be accepted or rejected by the community. Like Makkar (2002) I felt that, 'there was a sense of trust because I was being introduced by women...known to them' (p. 90). Nevertheless, the conditions for my acceptance were being defined and redefined as my relationships with different research participants were becoming multi-dimensional, fluid and ever changing over time. I was constantly engaged, both mentally and physically, in negotiating and re-negotiating my multiple identities while trying to keep my researcher identity intact (also see Ashraf in this volume for a discussion on similar issues).

The ethical dilemmas discussed so far arose due to tensions between the rules of ethical conduct and socio-cultural norms in the research context; former being the ethical standards created and agreed upon internationally, and being ethical environments which are locally defined and comprise unwritten 'rules' or locally acceptable ways of behaviour and interaction amongst the members of the community and with outsider 'guests'. Which rules should a researcher follow, when, where and why? These questions are dealt with in Part II.

Part II: A way forward

The ethical standards of research, under ethical universalism, are presented as universally applicable, objective and context free notions of right and wrong. The cultural pluralism view of ethics, on the other hand, is that there exist plural standards of right and wrong with elements of subjectivity and context specificity (see Levine, 1996 for more on this debate). An ethical environment is always context bound with its own standards of right and wrong and elements of subjectivity. More particularly, the ethical environment guides the researchers in how ethical issues should be handled in the field. Hence, a way forward for contexts like Pakistan needs to be located squarely within the pluralistic view of research ethics. Within this tradition, I agree with Simon and Usher's notion of 'situated-ness' of ethical decisions in a research context. For them, ethics 'is *situated* [emphasis in original]...local and specific...It cannot be universalized' (Simon and Usher, 2000). In the tradition of cultural pluralism in research ethics, I would qualify Simon and Usher's position as that of a 'complete cultural pluralism' because ascribing to this position indicates the need for local guidelines for researchers that are both contextually relevant and organic. These guidelines need to evolve and grow naturally in indigenous research environments. In the light of earlier discussion in Part I, it would seem appropriate to subscribe to the notion of ethics 'situated' in a context recognizing the complete cultural pluralism approach to ethics in research asking for 'local' and 'specific' guidelines. However, in the absence of a central academic body or organization with the designated task of designing codes for each research context, as in Pakistan, developing local ethical guidelines would be a challenge, to say the least. Moreover, the application of local standards only is problematic on many grounds. Firstly, it may lead to exploitation of local people by 'outsiders', who may justify their malpractices with reference to local ethical environment which they may not fully understand. Secondly, how local can we get because research context is not a singular entity; there are contexts within a context, both physically and theoretically, e.g. sub-cultures are present within what may broadly be described as the 'Pakistani culture'. Hence, we need to look at other ways of striking a balance between the international professional codes of ethics and the cultural norms and socio-cultural practices prevalent in diverse research contexts in developing countries such as Pakistan.

Taking the cultural pluralism perspective, Levine (1996) warns against the use of a standard set of general ethical guidelines for research: 'Any attempt to develop guidelines for ethical conduct must be grounded in a thorough and accurate understanding of the culture or cultures in which the guidelines are to be applied; otherwise, the guidelines will not accomplish their objectives' (p. 246). However, unlike Simons and Usher's

(2000) implied use of a 'stand alone' kind of local standards, Levine (1996) makes a case for recognizing 'the legitimacy of a limited degree of cultural pluralism' (p. 236) by improving international guidelines. I would define Levine's position as that of 'limited cultural pluralism'. This position suggests that international ethical standards can be treated as general principles, while 'the details of compliance with these broadly stated standards will be worked out on a case-by-case basis by ethical committees in the host country that have a high degree of understanding of the community in which the research is to be conducted' (Levine, 1996:245).

The position of limited cultural pluralism sounds like a marriage of convenience; nonetheless, it is worth considering on many accounts. Firstly, it would result in 'global' ethical guidelines. In Pakistan, (and similar contexts elsewhere) where a research culture is either absent or slowly emerging, in order to be at par with more developed research cultures, the established norms of the academia have to be followed. Developing a culture of academic debates and deliberations on ethical environmental concerns and application of international ethical standards is important for producing global guidelines because 'all ethical principles are developed in the course of discussions held within particular cultures…ethical principles are invented rather than discovered' (Levine, 1996:237).

Secondly, it accepts the situated-ness of research ethics by taking into account the ethical environment of different research contexts. By acknowledging the importance of ethical environment in formulating local and specific ethical guidelines, the limited cultural pluralism approach recognizes the specificity of particular research contexts which is denied by ethical universalism approach. Thirdly, it provides room for local participation in developing contextually relevant and professionally sound ethical codes for conducting research that are acceptable at both national and international levels. For instance, 'no harm to the participants' is an ethical principle agreed upon globally. However, the way it was enacted in the case of the two sisters in Pakistan, who almost became school drop outs, should be acceptable provided the researcher gives an account of the cultural context and reasons for interpreting or applying this principle in a particular way as was done in this specific research context. Fourthly, and perhaps the most important ground, is that the limited cultural pluralism position recognizes the importance of respecting local norms in conducting ethical research. Finally, this approach empowers indigenous people who can suggest ways to help future researchers working in 'local' settings whether as insider-outsider (see Ashraf and Asif in this volume) or as an outsider-insider (Pardhan in this volume and Pardhan, 2007). This also highlights the role of Ethics Review Committees in facilitating social science research in general and qualitative research in particular (Kliegman, Mahowald, Youngner and Pediatr, 1986; Lemmens and Freedman, 2000; Bhattacharya, 2007; Connolly and Reid, 2007).

Before I conclude, I would like to share an example of limited cultural pluralism in practice within the global singularism of ethical guidelines at the Aga Khan University (AKU), Karachi, Pakistan. The central Ethics Review Committee mainly comprises medical practitioners with representation from the university's Institute for Educational Development and civil society. The international ethical guidelines followed by AKU's Ethics Review Committee are the ones prepared by the Council for International Organizations of Medical Societies (CIOMS) in collaboration with the World Health Organization (WHO) and the Islamic Organization for Medical Sciences for Biomedical Research Involving Human Subjects. Being cognizant of the current debates on the issues associated with the applicability of the bioethical standards to social sciences even in the North (Israel, 2005; Israel and Hay, 2006), a local version of ethical guidelines for social sciences and humanities research has been developed by educationists from within the Aga Khan University for the Ethical Review Committee[8]. It is important to note that these guidelines have not replaced the universal, global ethical principles but are used in conjunction with the international guidelines for both medical and social sciences, but especially for social sciences.

AKU's Ethics Review Committee evaluates each case for ethical clearance under these guidelines but it does not take an 'audit approach to ethics clearance' (Connolly and Reid, 2007:1046) warranted by ethical universalism. Instead, when ground realities result in theoretical predicaments or field practices give rise to ethical dilemmas and field research deviates from the written guidelines, AKU-ERC invites the researcher(s) to explain clearly the context and rationale for doing so and the possible effects of such practice(s) on the validity and reliability of data. The researcher(s) is asked to document the process so as to make it transparent, on the one hand, and to help other researchers gain understanding of varied research contexts on the other. In this way, the ethical dilemmas that arise due to tensions between the ethical environment and ethical standards in research highlighted in Part I are immensely reduced, if not eliminated altogether.

Conclusion

Ethics has traditionally been seen as a set of general principles which can be applied in a range of situations. Research, when seen as a 'moral enterprise' (Vazir, 2004), may be more amenable to the application of universal and internationally acceptable ethical standards. This is the position of researchers/ethicists who adhere to 'ethical universalism' (Levine, 1996: 216). However, the conception of research as 'social practice, or more accurately a variety of social practices' (Simons and Usher, 2000:2), or a 'political process' (Vithal, 2008) defies such applications as socio-political interactions occur and take shape within an ethical environment and vary from context to context. Hence, research situations acquire different significance in diverse settings which may not be dealt effectively by 'one size fits all' set of rules and regulations provided by international ethical standards of research. Consequently, the position of cultural pluralism is beginning to gain support especially from social science research (see edited volumes by Simons and Usher, 2000; Welland and Pugsley, 2002). However, in this paper, I have argued that the limited cultural pluralism approach may help ease the tensions arising out of the interplay of ethical standards and ethical environments. This approach would allow researchers who wish to conduct qualitative research in different socio-cultural contexts in Pakistan, and elsewhere, to respect the ethical environment of their research context while abiding by the internationally developed and agreed upon ethical standards of research.

Notes

1. An earlier version of this paper titled; 'Whose ethics: Global guidelines and local realities' was presented at the Multidisciplinary International Conference on Qualitative Research in Developing Countries: Opportunities and challenges, at the University of Karachi Pakistan, 3–4 November 2006. The paper is also published in the Conference proceedings March 2007 (pp. 144–151).
2. Till recently, the author was associated with the Aga Khan University-Institute for Educational Development Karachi Pakistan as Assistant Professor. She can be contacted at her email address: rashidaqureshi_sm@yahoo.com
3. Higher Education Commission (HEC) in Pakistan is a recent development to promote research in higher education institutions. Although it is not functioning as IRB, it has taken note of the cases of plagiarism in higher education institutions in Pakistan. The Commission has developed a policy to investigate such cases and penalize the academics found to be guilty of the offense. It is expected that the Commission will be putting in place other monitoring mechanisms for ensuring high quality research is Pakistan.
4. It is one of the four provinces of Pakistan, now called Khyber Pakhtoonkhwa. It borders with Afghanistan and is considered to be more conservative than other parts of Pakistan.
5. A village council that takes decisions for entire village ranging from daily routine matters to cases related to criminal justice. The Jirga consists of all males, mostly village elders, and excludes both younger males and women. In many parts of Pakistan, the Jirga (or the equivalent of it) is still a dominant system for decision making at the local level.
6. See Miller and Bell (2005), 'Consenting to what? Issues of access, gate-keeping and 'informed' consent', in Mauthner, M, Birch, M, Jessop, J and

Miller, T (eds) *Ethics in Qualitative Research*, SAGE: London, pp. 53–69, for a detailed discussion of similar issues.

7. For example see the guidelines for publishing in ABRA or TESOL.
8. These guidelines are available on the university's website. http://akuied/ied/raps/Documents/ERCPoliciesGuidelines.pdf

References

Bhattacharya, K., 'Consenting to the Consent Form: What are the Fixed and Fluid Understandings between the Researcher and the Researched?' *Qualitative Inquiry*, 13 (2007) 1095–1115.

Blackburn, S., *Being Good: A Short Introduction to Ethics* (Oxford: Oxford University Press, 2001).

Corrigan, O., 'Empty Ethics: the Problem with Informed Consent', *Sociology of Health & Illness*, 25 (7) (2003), 768–792.

Connolly, K., and Reid, A., 'Ethics Review for Qualitative Inquiry: Adopting a Value-based, Facilitative Approach', *Qualitative inquiry*, 13 (2007), 1031–1047.

Eisner, E.W., *The Enlightened Eye* (USA: Prentice Hall, 1998).

Government of Pakistan, *Pakistan Economic Survey: 2004–2005* (Government of Pakistan: Islamabad, 2005).

Halai, A., *Role of social interactions in students' learning of mathematics (in classrooms in Pakistan)*, Ph.D. dissertation (UK: Oxford University, 2001).

Israel, M., 'Research Hamstrung by Ethics Creep', *The Australian Higher Education Supplement* (12 January 2005).

Israel, M., and Hay, L., *Research Ethics for Social Scientists* (CA: Sage publications, 2006).

Khan, T.S., *Beyond Honour: A Historical Materialist Explanation of Honour Related Violence* (Pakistan: Oxford University Press, 2008).

Kliegman, R.M., Mahowald, M.B., Youngner, S.J, and Pediatr, J., 'In Our Best Interest: Experience and Working of an Ethics Review Committee', *British Medical Journal*, 108 (2) (1986), 178–88.

Lemmens, T., and Freedman, B., 'Ethics review for sale? Conflict of Interest and Commercial Research Review Boards', *Milbank Quarterly*, <pt.wkhealth.com.>, accessed 2000.

Levine, R.J., 'International Codes and Guidelines for Research Ethics: A Critical Appraisal', <http://www.columbia.akadns.net/itc/hs/pubhealth/p9740/readings/levine.pdf>, accessed on 31 December 2008.

Makkar, B.D., 'Roles and Responsibilities in Researching Poor Women in Brazil', in T. Welland and L. Pugsley (eds.), *Ethical Dilemmas in Qualitative Research* (UK: Ashgate, 2002), 75–93.

Pardhan, A., 'Methodological Issues and Tensions: Reflections on Conducting Ethnographic Research with Women in Booni Valley, Chitral District,

Pakistan', in R. Qureshi and J.F. Rarieya (eds.), *Gender and Education in Pakistan* (Karachi: Oxford University Press, 2007).

Pugsley, L., 'Putting Your Oar In: Moulding, Muddling or Meddling?', in T. Welland and L. Pugsley (eds.), *Ethical dilemmas in Qualitative Research* (Aldershot: Ashgate, 2002), 19–31.

Qureshi, R., 'Colonial Legacy: Understanding the Historical Roots of Female Illiteracy in Pakistan', *Muslim Education Quarterly*, 23 (1 & 2) (2006), 20–37.

Roberts, L.W., 'Informed Consent and the Capacity for Voluntarism', *American Journal of Psychiatry*, 159 (2002), 705–712.

Roberts, L., and Roberts, B., 'Psychiatric Research Ethics: An Overview of Evolving Guidelines and Current Ethical Dilemmas in the Study of Mental Illness', *Biological Psychiatry*, 46 (1999), 1025–38.

Simons H., and Usher, R. (eds.), *Situated Ethics in Educational Research* (London: Routledge, 2000).

Shamim, F., 'Teacher-learner Behaviour and Classroom Processes in Large ESL Classes in Pakistan', Ph.D. dissertation (School of Education, University of Leeds, UK, 1993).

Strike, K.A., Anderson, M.S., Curren, R., Geel, T.V., Pritchard, I., and Robertson, E., *Ethical Standards of the American Educational Research Association: Cases and Commentary* (Washington, DC: American Educational Research Association, 2002).

Tully, J., Ninis, N., Booy, R. and Viner, R., 'The New System of Review by Multicentre Research Ethics Committees: Prospective Study', *British Medical Journal*, 320 (2000), 1179–1182.

Vazir, N., 'Research Ethics: Significance, Application and Obligation to the Practice of Research', *Journal of Educational Research*, 7(1/2) (2004), 3–11.

Vithal, R., 'Research Methodologies in the "South"', Key note address at the two-day conference on 'Research Methodologies in the "South"', AKU, Karachi, Pakistan (3–4 December 2008).

Welland, T.S., and Pugsley, L. (eds.), *Ethical Dilemmas in Qualitative Research*, (Aldershot: Ashgate, 2002).

Acknowledgement

I wish to acknowledge the contribution of all my friends, colleagues and graduate students who took part in the development of this paper by sharing their ethical dilemmas with me. I am grateful to Dr Fauzia Shamim and Ms Rahat Joldoshalieva for their review of earlier drafts of this paper and their valuable comments. Above all I wish to thank all boys and girls, and men and women, whose interaction with me and my fellow researchers brought humanness into an otherwise detached and cold scientific endeavour.

Section III

Qualitative Research in the South:
Focus on Methodology

5

Using a feminist standpoint for researching women's lives in the rural mountainous areas of Pakistan

DILSHAD ASHRAF

Introduction

Feminist research is rooted in the view that 'all knowledge claims are socially located and that some locations, especially those at the bottom of social and economic hierarchies, are better than others as starting points for seeking knowledge not only about those particular women but others as well' (Olesen, 2003: 343). Women's position within sexual division of labour and their experiences of oppression are perceived as granting women a leverage to develop insights into women's experiences as researchers (Hartstock as cited in Hesse-Biber and Yaiser, 2004). While feminist scholarship, according to Hesse-Biber and Yaiser (2004), varies in epistemological positions and research, a feminist approach to research helps give voice to the experiences, concerns, attitudes and needs of women. The study I undertook to explore women teachers' life histories was theoretically and practically positioned in this feminist premise in research. I examined how my research participants, i.e. women teachers, combined their traditional familial role and their role as professionals in a patriarchal society that has seen a gradual shift from subsistence agriculture economy to cash economy. Considering the patriarchal nature of the research context, there was a desire to view these differences in social positions from the women teachers' perspective. This knowledge, I believed, would be more relevant and credible as resulting from an attempt to see knowledge and reality from the 'social position of women as a privileged vantage point from which to view social reality' (Haig, 1999: 226). The research revealed that the shift from subsistence agriculture economy to the cash economy has implicated gender relationship with a significant expansion of women's traditional familial role of care giving while men have sustained their roles as family and community elders.

Life history as research methodology has become popular among feminist researchers (e.g. Blackmore, 1999; Britzman, 1991; Casey, 1993; Hall, 1996, Munro, 1998; Weiler, 1998) who have used it to explore women teachers' and leaders' experiences and to understand how these women make sense of their struggle. Agreeing with Munro's (1998) statement that 'all meanings are culturally and historically contingent; meanings are created by and in social life' (p. 2), I concluded that a combination of life history and a feminist view would grant me the opportunity to undertake 'provocative and productive unpacking of taken-for-granted ideas about women in specific material, historical, and cultural contexts' (Olesen, 2000: 215). The research context (the Northern Areas of Pakistan), being my native region, also bore methodological implications for a feminist study and required a more reflexive methodology which offers opportunities for raising new questions and engaging in new kinds of dialogue (Hesse-Biber and Piatelli, 2007). Hesse-Biber and Piatelli (2007) define reflexivity as a self-critical action whereby the researcher is mediated by the self- what can be known can be known through oneself, one's lived experiences and one's biography. This self-critical action, as an act of reflexivity, warranted my personal experiences of life to shape the content and method of the research that aimed at exploring women's experiences of juggling their various roles. A retrospective analysis of my experience of researching reveals tension between conventional researching practices, local cultures and my feminist standpoint. This chapter captures nuances from my research as it was implicated by the feminist approach of reflexivity. In particular, the methodological and ethical tensions and challenges that were closely associated with my position as a local feminist researcher researching life histories of local women are discussed. The discussion is organized around two major themes, i.e. methodological and ethical tensions. This provides a ground for exploring possibilities and challenges of conducting life history research with a feminist perspective in the patriarchal context of the Northern Areas of Pakistan.

Theoretical perspective

The study itself resides in the standpoint of feminist theory according to which the epistemic privilege is often accorded to the standpoint of women and/or other oppressed people. A standpoint, according to Hartstock (as cited in Sprague and Kobrynowicz, 2004), is not obvious; it is mediated and based on one's position in the achieved social order rather than immediate understanding. The premise of standpoint theory is that a hierarchical society will produce different standpoints, or vantage points, from which social life is experienced. That also means that structural difference creates difference in experiences and beliefs (Hesse-Biber, Leavy and Yaiser, 2004).

As a research approach, feminist view offers a response to conventional research that seems to maintain a hierarchical power relationship grounded in the sharp distinction between researchers and researched. Feminist research aims at promoting relationship of closeness, connectedness and caring as opposed to researcher possessing control over the researched. The researcher's goal is to give voice to women [and/or other oppressed] to express their experience in their terms (Sprague & Kobrynowicz, 2004). Feminists (such as Hartstock, 1983) emphasize the importance of women's location within the sexual division of labour and their experience of oppression in enabling women researchers develop greater insights into the lives of other women. It implies that a way of knowing must start from women's lives as women researchers' own understanding and experiences have implications for creating knowledge (Smith,

1999 as cited in Hesse-Biber, Leavy and Yaiser, 2004). This standpoint has guided my study both conceptually and methodologically. Some of my experiences of conducting feminist research are presented in the forthcoming sections of the chapter. The experiences related to methodology and ethical dimensions are dealt under separate headings.

Research Methodology

Munro (1998) calls the process of recovering women's voices as 'invisible mending' (p. 6) which she thought could be best done through using life history research. Hence, I chose life history as a research methodology to explore experiences of five women teachers in the rural mountain country in Pakistan. To enrich my data, I also observed my research participants in both workplace and home settings. In this, section, I discuss the tensions and dilemmas that emerged from my methodological decisions.

Life History Interviews

Interviewing is consistent with many women's interest in avoiding control over others and developing a sense of connectedness (Reinharz, 1992: 20). Interviewing may allow women to be actively engaged in constructing data about their lives to avoid alienation of the research from the researched. My feminist stance of researching women's experiences from 'their privileged vantage point' (Haig, 1999: 226) called for questioning Seidman's famous model (1998) of a three-interview series for life history research. He suggests that the first interview facilitates participants' ability to reconstruct their early experiences related to their families, friends, and workplace. The second interview concentrates on particular details of the first interview that relate to the research issue, while the third interview elicits the meanings of the research participants' experiences. Research participants while sharing their experiences decided the sequence of their life stories that were not necessarily chronological.

Throughout, they were engaged in making meaning of their experiences. Besides, using this model required extended time for each of the three interviews which participants, with their intense professional and familial commitments, could not spare. Therefore, the flow of interviews was determined by participants' availability and the sequence of the events chosen by them. In line with standpoint feminist position, to get participants' views on how they sequence their life experiences, the study provided the participants the choice of time which resulted in interviews of varied duration (some interviews lasted only 30 minutes while others lasted about one to two hours).

The life history interviews in the study constantly took the form of a dialogue between the participants and me, facilitating the reconstruction and interpretation of subjectively meaningful features and critical episodes (Creswell, 1998; Denzin, 1989) in our individual lives. Occasionally, I shared with research participants my own life experiences and turning points, complying with the feminist principle of 'reciprocity in research'. Discussions about critical episodes or life's turning points proved a journey of self-discovery that explicated my association with other women teachers of the area in general, and my research participants, in particular. For instance, Fatima and I shared the grief of losing a child, which provided me a sense of association with her. The inter-subjective process of meaning making took place in a collaborative fashion and we together felt that our attempts to make our decisions at times proved to be radical actions. For instance, my decision of leaving my newborn with my mother in order to continue my higher education and Fatima's decision of working as radio artists were received by our communities as dissident acts. Munro (1998) suggests that the process of understanding another woman's life is one of empathy and identification. The process of identification or connection, according to Munro (1998), makes the subjective experiences central to understanding them [teachers] and writing their life stories. A retrospective analysis of my interactions with Fatima and other participants reveals that my connection with the participants in part depended on revealing researcher's own stories—an enactment of feminist research principle of reciprocity and shared meaning making.

Observation

The 'shared cultural perspective' (Shah, 2004: 552) I had of women's social position in the patriarchal society led me to view the limitations of using only life history interviews for data collection. I was aware that the embeddedness of patriarchy as a social structure could constrain women teachers' attempts to recognize the distinctive nature of their everyday experiences. Therefore, I searched for other ethnographic methods for generating data on women's experiences to broaden the scope of our inter-subjective process of meaning making. Observing women teachers in the context of the lives they lived with their multiple identities, I felt, could enrich the data collected through life history interviews. Furthermore, observation was envisaged to help 'establish as broad a context as possible for understanding the life histories' (Munro, 1998: 11) of women teachers. As participant and non-participant observer, I observed them not only teaching their students but also interacting with colleagues, head teachers, staff, parents, and others within the school environment. My position as insider would have made it difficult to be 'a fly on the wall' and hence necessitated the use of participant observation. My image of an aloof researcher could create suspicion among teachers who could relate to me with multiple references. I, therefore, avoided demonstration of such an image and used appropriate data collection methods to know the participants and earn their trust as a qualitative researcher (Bogdan and Biklen, 2007; Maykut and Morehouse, 1994).

Participant observation allowed me to enter the women's lives and to understand them while suspending, as much as possible, my own view of their world. Observing the participants, I took positions from insider (knowing it all) to outsider (observing keenly from a distance). Creswell (1998) rightly postulates that participant observation offers possibilities for the researcher to be on a continuum from being a complete outsider to being a complete insider. At times, I looked at their taken-for-granted experiences from an outsider perspective, while at other times, I reflected on their lives with an insider's perspective. For instance, while observing Zehra and Fatima conducting meetings with members of their Women's Organizations (WOs), I observed and reflected on their interactions with other women and with each other. As manager of a WO in my own village, I had been engaged in a number of such meetings, but had never thought of the implications for women who attended the meetings and for myself. In addition to this, I felt that my observation of the participants explicated implicit knowledge of particular aspects of their different roles which they never expressed during formal or informal talks with me. For instance, while observing Fatima at home, I understood the level of her relationship with the women members of her WO. A young woman entered the kitchen while Fatima was making bread. This woman told Fatima that she also wanted membership in the organization and she left some money for Fatima to process her membership. Fatima promised to do that and also invited her to join the family for lunch that she was busy preparing. At that time, I was waiting for Fatima's reaction to the situation (the woman had invaded her private time). This was a 'researchable moment' for me to understand how she perceived community involvement. Fatima remained very patient; later the concern raised by Fatima with regard to the pressure of community development took me back to the time when I spent hours waiting for the members of Village Women Organization for meetings and for processing their monthly savings. Being cognizant of the constraints that women of my village face in terms of economical credentials, I endured the pressure on my time and energy. Observing women engaged in negotiating their space in community provided us with an opportunity to come together in a dialogue. Together we discussed the opportunities these forums had provided to the women of the area. An analysis of our work as the manager of our respective women's village organizations also explicated our contribution to the gradually occurring social change in the Northern Areas.

The retrospective analysis of my engagement in the post observation dialogic natured conversations signifies the importance of observation as a data collection strategy for a feminist researcher, particularly in patriarchal societies. Observations in such a context have the capability to further the purpose of life history research which, according to some life historians (e.g. Goodson & Sikes, 2001; Munro, 1998), is a) to explicate ways of negotiating identities and making sense of the social world and; b) to explore the dialectical relationship between the self and society. Furthermore, a combination of life history interview and observations (with post observation dialogue), in the examples quoted earlier, can lead to reflectiveness and consciousness-raising, the two attributes of life history research recognized by Huberman (1995).

Methodological tensions in researching women's experiences

Negotiating positions

The consent of five women teachers regarding their participation in the study was, from the onset, 'a dynamic relationship rather than a static decision' (Smith 1999: 136). The women teachers believed that their participation in the research was their obligation to a sister (me), the very first woman doctoral candidate from the area, who by doing doctoral studies, was a role model for the women in the area. This belief seemed as much their feminist commitment as was the feminist researcher's claim of providing marginalized roles a central place in the world of knowledge. Thus the process of constructing the research relationship of mutuality between five women and me (the researcher) provided opportunity for explicating connectedness, self-revelation and emotional support to voice and interpret our taken for granted experiences (Cook, Fonow and Oakley cited in Sprague and Kobrynowicz, 2004).

The trust that these women teachers demonstrated in my role as researcher was grounded in our shared affiliation with the mountain communities as local women. For this reason, none of them initially showed any concern about the content of the consent letter. It was only towards the end of my fieldwork that one of my research participants asked me if I would also disguise the name of her village. Being an insider, I was concerned about the participants' vulnerability in this particular context with close knit communities, where the unique patterns of their individual life experiences are well known to everyone in that community. Her underlying fear added to my sensitivity on how I would report my study.

Generally, 'like all other relationships, the researcher-participants relationship is subject to continuing negotiation and reworking; this extends to the participants' trust in the researcher's behaviour and integrity at every stage of research' (Darlington and Scott, 2002: 54). Since I knew some of the participants, the development of my relationship with all five participants varied initially. However, the close affinity that developed between us was based on months of fieldwork, which helped us share our similar backgrounds and aims in life, i.e. to be effective members of the community and family, to earn an independent living, and to further our children's education. My identity as a local woman, educator, and fellow teacher enhanced my role as a researcher. Though I kept my research agenda up front, the participants were not ready to reconcile to it and identified with their 'preferred' identity of me. They called me 'our sister' and confided in me to the extent that I worried about the ethical obligations towards the vulnerability of the participants. Shortly thereafter, our relationship developed in which my presence for the five women became a part of the whole scenario of a close network of relationships. By fitting into this pattern, I achieved what Berg (2001: 148) calls 'erosion of visibility by display of symbolic attachment'. Berg explains that a researcher can, 'become invisible because their informants suspend concern over the research aspect of their identity in favour of liking the researcher as a person'. Considering me a sister was the participants' attempt to position me according to the norms of their particular society where every individual is placed in reference to a blood and ethnic relationship. My identity as a 'sister' led them to place me in their family circle; thus I qualified for a more intimate relationship.

Women's ways of knowing, recognizing, and building relationships are unique in the indigenous culture of the mountain communities. Intricacies of maintaining relationships around births, deaths, and local festivities within extended families and clan depend on women to women contacts. In particular, relationship between women provides a base for social structures that range from extended families to clan systems. The development of my relationship with my research participants, on one hand, was informed by the feminist perspective on research; on the other hand, it was directed by indigenous culture of care—the core value in the web of relationship in the local culture. As my research proceeded, I developed more insights into the participants' family life and at times extended my cooperation as needed. For instance, I helped Fatima respond to job advertisements for her daughter, who had just completed her Master's degree. The daughter luckily got the job for which I had forwarded her application. Another time, during my visit to her family, I found that Fatima's daughter in Grade 7 came home from school with a high fever. Knowing the transportation problem in the area, I offered to take them to the nearest health centre to get proper medication. Small acts of taking somebody to the doctor or giving them a ride to the market, I believe, demonstrated my sensitivity to the issues in their daily lives. This eventually took the form of reciprocity. Being an insider, I tried to keep up with the practices of our culture which places a lot of importance on developing a sense of belongingness and reciprocity. When visiting the participants' families, I always took with me a small gift such as a cake or cookies in compliance with the norms of local culture. In return, they insisted on my taking home with me fresh vegetables or fruit, knowing that I did not have enough land and skills to grow vegetables. The relationship of reciprocity was further enhanced when we shared our life experiences with one another. The knowledge of our life experiences allowed us to collaborate in making meaning of our taken for granted interactions which at times face rejections by the society as *'gus gias-e-chaghaming'*, an expression in Brushaski language shared by the four participants and myself. This expression literally means 'women and children talk' underlining the insignificance seen in a woman's point of view or her interaction with other women. Demystification of these long standing gendered views happened through our exploratory engagement in making meaning of our experiences. The purpose of this knowledge was empowerment, enabling us to undertake some purposive action in the societies we embodied. It was an important learning that telling the stories of our experiences could be personally empowering, supporting mutual empathy and feelings of connectedness.

At times, I gave up my research agenda to help my research participants teach. For instance, my field notes of my visits to Zehra's school and classes were shorter because I began teaching with her rather than writing the field notes. Upon finding her struggling to teach a mathematical concept, I decided to assist her resolve the issue. We planned a lesson, developed materials, and taught together in the class. This act of mine was rooted in my understanding of the constraints she had in developing her professional knowledge and skills. Prolonged stay in the research context also intensified the ethical stance of maintaining confidentiality. This was particularly challenged in the context of my relationship with others with whom I had developed acquaintanceship by virtue of multiple references (e.g. far off relative, belonging to the same clan, past reference of a teaching workshop). Constant queries made me guard what Burgess (1984: 203) called as 'oral communication of data' by not publicly talking about my research. Some of the participants' colleagues inquired about my activities in the participants' classes and homes. My response that I was 'trying to understand their lives' was not very satisfactory. To avoid further queries, I downplayed my research agenda while sitting with the teachers during their recess get together. My preferable reference point was talking around the challenges of teaching or the weather, the topics that concerned the majority of teachers. Hence, my efforts to maintain relationship with the participants, in the words of Darlington and Scott (2002), were subject to continuing negotiation and reworking. Here, my integrity as a researcher, I believe, was guided by the women's indigenous ways of building relationships and recognizing them as much, as it was directed by feminist research ethics and conventional norms of researching.

Negotiating research and indigenous culture

A retrospective analysis of my experience of researching women's lives reveals a tension between conventional researching practices, local culture and my feminist standpoint. As mentioned earlier, I observed the participants in different settings (school, home, meetings in relation to participants' community development work). In these observations, I constantly moved positions on the continuum of participant to non-participant observer. Observations at home were particularly meant to see how the female teachers were engaged in their different responsibilities at home and also how they related to the members of their extended families. In general, according to Reinharz (1992: 68), 'feminist participant observation values openness to intimacy and striving for empathy, which should not be confused with superficial friendship. Rather it means openness to complete transformation or consciousness-raising'. My plan of spending more than two hours in the homes of my research participants, with a built-in post-observation discussion did not work out, as I had overlooked the impracticality of this idea in a culture that is well known for hospitality and the value given to guests.

To keep my profile low as a guest, I urged all my research participants not to inform their families about my expected visits. This was done to save the families from the trouble of making special arrangement to receive a guest at home. In three cases, the older family members, especially the mothers-in-law disapproved of the participants' not sharing the plan of my visit with their respective families. Particularly, the 'head women' in two instances expressed their discontent in my presence. I realized that my attempt to keep a low profile had, in fact, led to the families' discomfort as they were unable to entertain me according to the standards of indigenous hospitality. During home visits, I was made to sit in the best room of the house and was served the best food, including meat, while the participants were busy in the kitchen.

Though observing the women in their home situations enhanced both my awareness and curiosity about the interactions going on around them in different environments, my visits to their homes changed the whole scenario of their everyday home lives. I realized that all the family members were alert and every day routines were altered to accommodate my visit. For example, on one occasion, I stayed with my research participant Khadija in a village in Ghizar District. Khadija and I, with our different ethnic backgrounds, were residents of two different districts that have different languages and to some extent different cultures. I stayed with her not only to collect rich data but also to avoid staying alone in a hotel, which is an uncommon and unacceptable option for women in that area. During this visit too I kept to the objective of my visit, that is, to observe my research participants as they engaged in their familial responsibilities. However, Khadija took time off from her core household chores to spend time with me. Her unmarried younger sister came to help her and took over all the household chores usually done by Khadija in the afternoons, enabling Khadija to keep me company. Khadija took me around the land they had bought in recent years and also took me to her parents' house. Acquiring land had been a significant family achievement in Khadija's life and that of her family. It gave them the status of an affluent household, which they did not have earlier due to their possessing a small piece of land that was inherited by Khadija's father-in-law. Possessing land and its significance became clear to me when Khadija took me around, proudly showing her family-owned land. Her narrative of earlier struggles of the family gave me a new perspective on diversity of women's experiences within the same region. Keeping in view my apprehensions of staying in a hotel, Khadija and her family accommodated me in their home despite centuries old regional differences. In the past, Hunza (my origin) and Ghizar (Khadija's origin) were among many small independent princely states which were part of an on-going regional feud. Although the practical animosity between the two states disappeared after the government of Pakistan abolished the former monarchies in 1970, the sense of being different still prevails. Khadija's subsequent visit to my home in Hunza further brought us into the fold of a feminist relationship.

In my research context, having an easy access to the participants' lives as a feminist and as an insider called for intense scrutiny. My status as a doctoral candidate in a foreign university, and an exposure to higher education and a different life style, had placed me in an outsider's position. Conversing in the mother tongue also exposed my inadequate language proficiency— another evidence of my urban upbringing. This further strengthened my position as an outsider. Smith (1999) experienced the same dilemma while researching in her native tribe. Her status as a researcher, with exposure to university, with a monthly income and even a car, contributed to making her an outsider. I remained an outsider, despite having what Shah calls (2004: 559) 'social access' and 'shared culture'. My identity of a local female teacher did not guarantee my unconditional entry into the private lives of the extended families of my research participants. As a novice researcher, I also developed some insights into real-life research, and the problems of applying a research concept developed mainly in the North American context in the remote, indigenous culture of the Northern Areas in Pakistan. The most important dimension of this scenario was self doubt for my inability, as a feminist researcher, to recognize research participants' and my own social position within a culture of care and hospitality which sometimes led to culturally inappropriate conduct on my part. I realized that a researcher cannot be an insider even in one's own culture. In fact, it made me recognize the inherent multiplicity of researcher roles warranted by various factors such as 'power relations, gender, age, class, knowledge, profession' which Shah (2004: 564) believes are important considerations for conducting research in a monocultural context such as that of a rural mountain country in Northern Pakistan.

Research as a revealing journey in my world

My relationship with the participants' social world was a fundamental asset for research. This asset, at times, necessitated intense engagement of reflection beyond the required depth for research. As my research progressed, I had frequent discussions with women representing different spheres of social life. Each encounter with the participants, other women teachers, and women working in different capacities, confirmed and reaffirmed their multidimensional struggle as they worked through their routine activities. I tried to understand our mutual patriarchal society from their eyes as well as through reflecting on my own taken-for-granted experiences. A closer and more critical look at the society in general, and the education system and schools as work place for female teachers in particular, revealed that many women were not able to recognize the oppression confronting them in their respective social positions. My recognition of the interplay of the patriarchal system and 'taken for granted' experiences of women can be explained with an example. A female teacher shared that she was sponsored by the school system (her employer) to participate in a one-year teacher training programme in a local institution in town. She moved with her young children and her father-in-law to live closer to the training institution. Soon there was a disagreement between her husband and the education officer, who was instrumental in sending her for the training, as the husband wanted his wife to stop attending the training program, due to the difficulties she was facing in living in town with young children. The female teacher considered the education officer at fault because of his insistence on her continuing the training despite his knowing that she was a mother and had to take care of her children and family. Eventually, she discontinued the training and has not found such an opportunity again. Her retrospective analysis did not indicate an understanding of her subjugation by the two male members of the patriarchal society; none allowed her to exercise her right to decide the course of her personal and professional life. She was forced to enrol and later withdraw from a professional course without her consent. Yet she seemed to accept this subjugation as a given in her socio-cultural context. My process of meaning-making was thus contingent upon the cultural and historical context (Munro, 1998). The following memo in my reflective journal illustrates this process:

> Occasionally, I feel that my independent position as a researcher has made people in my research context open up about issues they are unable to discuss with their officials. Although I am rowing my research boat with two oars (insider, outsider), my position as an insider keeps me overwhelmed. I have experienced conflict between my various identities; identity of a female, identity of a teacher, and my feminist researcher identity. Often, a temptation of getting engaged in resolving apparent gender disparities in the workplace of women and within society at large surfaces strongly.
>
> (Memo, 18 July 2002)

Berg's (1989) view of humane perspective in research along with my feminist position made the research experience a revealing journey in the world I had always lived in. The lack of inquiry among young girls of Grade 8 provided sufficient reason for my distress as they did not inquire from their teacher about the purpose of my regular visits to their class. Questioning them for not asking questions about me could have been termed as 'social intrusion' (Shah, 2004: 565). As an insider, it was almost impossible to separate my female self from my research agenda. In a workshop on women teachers' experiences, my spontaneous reaction to my colleagues' inability to recognize how patriarchal values and interests governed their lives surprised them as they had so far seen me as only as a quiet observer. I felt that with my research agenda I could help 'us' recharge our spirits as women of a new age, seeking a new space—identifying a fine line between relationships of respect and care and domination and oppression.

A retrospective analysis of the above dilemmas has helped me place 'lives of women teachers within a broader [social] historical context in which these women lived' (Munro, 1998: 11). The depth of analysis of women teachers' experiences that I associated partly to my insider position also indicates a reflection of transformative and conscious raising nature of feminist research. The process of transformation and consciousness raising, nevertheless, has to begin with the researcher's constant efforts to understand women's position in the social fabric. This requires developing a 'clear sense of social and political processes through which our experiences are constructed' (Wilkinson, 2004: 285). This understanding along with the position of an 'insider' has the potential to allow feminist researchers like me to explain the transformative dimension of women's experiences. The earlier discussion about methodological dilemmas reinforces the idea of self reflexivity. I constantly asked myself about my own position as a feminist local researcher that led to many unanswered queries about reconciling the conventional research methods with a sense of indigenous context. Strong reflexivity, according to Harding (cited in Hesse-Bibber and Leckenby, 2004: 219), is 'a process whereby researchers take a critical look at their conceptual schema or the frameworks that comprise their social locations'. In other words, reflexive feminist researchers explore their own values and the assumptions that they bring to their research and how these values and assumption may impact the questions they want to address in their research. In line with Hesse-Bibber and Leckenby (2004), I saw the value of reflexivity during various stages of research experiences including data collection, analysis, and writing. Such understanding of a reflexive stance can enhance the feminist life history researchers' opportunities to undertake research projects in indigenous communities elsewhere in the world.

Ethical considerations in researching women's experiences

Researching human beings is an extremely sensitive task, which should be undertaken with fairness and ethically appropriate attitudes by the researcher. Hence, research in the social sciences is essentially an ethical endeavour, raising social and moral obligations (Punch, 1994). For both the researcher and the researched, 'relationships are delicate and labile, and must be nurtured if the research is to continue' (Brickhouse, 1992: 96). The delicacy of relationships adds to the researcher's obligations to always 'be cognizant that ethical responsibilities are not over when initial consent is obtained—they are just beginning' (ibid.). A discussion on the interactions between conventional researching methods and ethics and values of local culture is presented in this section.

A researcher with an indigenous identity, pursuing a research project that involves indigenous participants, from the very outset becomes more vulnerable in the struggle to respect indigenous ethics while combining them with conventional research ethics. In line with the content of reflexivity, my insider position as a local female required me to be more critical of the research processes I was employing in the context of my own people and culture. Smith (1999) postulates that insider research has to be as ethical and respectful, and as reflexive and critical as outsider research. It also needs to be humble, because the researcher belongs to the community as a member with a different set of roles and relationships, status, and position.

My status as a highly educated woman put me in a powerful position with my research participants. To eliminate the effects of my being an 'outsider' with exceptional credentials (relative to other women), I tried to keep a low profile by not identifying myself with the hierarchy of the system and society. Following my fellow feminist researcher Casey (1993), I took on the ethical obligations of developing a relationship of reciprocity and respect for the 'authenticity' and 'integrity' of my research participants' narrations. To avoid becoming a coaxer (Plummer, 1983), it was my undertaking to encourage women without voice to develop an 'increased self knowledge' (Brickhouse, 1992: 97) and to acknowledge the worth of their life experiences. From time to time, I provided them with professional support and also invited them to celebrate our worthiness as women in this patriarchy and demystify the prevailing myth of the deficit model of women (Acker, 1994). This was done through revisiting their 'taken for granted' experiences and by viewing them with feminist lenses. I was conscious of becoming an intruder and kept in mind weather conditions and the intensity of seasonal farming work prior to visiting their homes; to avoid any inconvenience, the visits were negotiated in advance.

My research endeavor was sophisticated; it aimed at encouraging women to voice their own experiences and their own interpretations of these experiences. It involved women in a process of research that they had never experienced before. Therefore, at the outset, I discussed with the participants my research, its focus, and specifically its possible outcomes and implications. Their participation in the research was recognized by the women teachers, as mentioned earlier, as their obligation to a sister. Shah (2004) refers to a situation like mine as collective cultures which have a perspective of interpersonal responsibility and moral duty to individuals. This responsibility leads the research participants to oblige individuals who are seen as part of the community. Despite the teachers' persistent expression of their obligation to me, in the framework of indigenous sisterhood, I fulfilled my ethical obligations by reading with them the contents of the consent letter before they signed it.

After developing a relationship with the research participants, my ethical obligation to guard their personal information that they shared with me intensified. The problem of confidentiality was particularly important in my research. I felt quite uneasy promising complete confidentiality, which seemed difficult to fulfil. My presence in the participants' schools was very obvious to their colleagues and students. Attempts to maintain confidentiality, however, were endangered by the participants who disclosed their 'work with me'. Upholding the research ethics of confidentiality and anonymity in this unique context with multiple terms of reference was a challenging task. Researching relationship, among all other relationships, seemed to be less important. They happily acknowledged 'our sister', thereby risking confidentiality through their action of doing away with my ethical stance.

The ethical obligations towards avoiding the elements of directives and reactivity (Glesne & Peshkin, 1992) posed another dilemma to my insider feminist identity. The frequent response of one of the participants 'what can I say about it?' left me in a quandary. As an insider, I felt I knew the answers to many of my questions but was eager to know the participants' responses. By positioning my research as life history research with a feminist perspective, I was searching for the participants' voices and the interpretations of their experiences. Hence, I was caught up in ethical and methodological dilemmas during my interaction with them.

Ethics refer to the question of values, that is, of 'beliefs, judgments, and personal viewpoints' (Hitchcock and Hughes, 1995: 44). Values vary from one context to another. Thus, the question arises as to whether ethics should be dogmatically applied or the researcher's ethical considerations should take into account the political context of the research (Bibby, 1997). My research context, 'the Northern Areas of Pakistan', has its own cultural values. At times, I felt a clash between these contextual values, my methodological needs and the detachment suggested by the application of conventional research ethics. For instance, while discussing turning points in our lives, I probed into an important phase of Fatima's life, when her son and mother had died within the span of a few months. This tragedy was already known to me as she had mentioned it to me earlier. Now I wanted to probe further into that aspect of her experience. However, she avoided talking about them as 'dead'. I felt she was attempting to avoid the grief she had experienced. Contextually, there seemed to be another rationale for her behaviour. There is a norm of sharing grief with the family of the deceased during the first 7 to 40 days. During this period, the relatives and neighbours remain with the family of the deceased to provide physical and emotional support. Once the initial rites are over, the family is expected to develop the courage to bear that loss, accepting it as God's will. To 'enrich' my data, I probed into this phase of Fatima's life and made her talk about it. My own experience of losing a child brought us closer, because we shared this experience. However, I realized that it was equally difficult for me to talk about my loss, because both of us had been brought up in the same culture. Probing for the research-required data was emotionally stressful for the participant and for me as it did not conform to the norms and culture of our indigenous society. While this critical episode posed an ethical dilemma for me, sharing Fatima's grief and seeing how it strengthened her was an important element of this feminist discourse.

Principle of visibility and reporting dilemmas

The earlier accounts of feminist researchers' experiences indicate that the researcher is as much an active agent as the participant. Hence, acknowledging individual agency is important for restructuring the power relationship between the researcher and the research participants. The choices being made by the researcher are shaped and motivated by social location from the choice of a research topic to decisions on how to present the material. Reporting a person's life history in the form of a reflective text is a challenging task for the researcher. This involves vulnerable and voiceless research participants, because the researcher has both power and control over the process of writing (Kay, 1998). Though, as a feminist researcher, I claimed to maintain the principle of reciprocity and tried to eliminate power patterns with my research participants, the ultimate decision and authority of how to present the research rested with me. The risk involved in an insider's research was quite evident and, therefore, demanded vigilance in maintaining the participants' voice 'up front' in my writing. My desire of creating a reflective text to enable readers make sense of unheard voices and make connections between the multiple voices of the told lives also stood contested. Such text, I believe, would be accessible to a mixed audience of both academics and the people in my research context. This accessibility, I knew, would make me and the participants vulnerable even if I present the stories of my research participants behind a shield of anonymity (Christians, 2000; Tierney, 2000). However, Tierney (2000) argues that this vulnerability is not a position of weakness, but one with which to attempt change and social fellowship. The decision on how to present the life histories of these five women teachers presented a dilemma. Knowing and living the vulnerable position of these women participants, I decided to bring together objective and subjective markers (Denzin, 1989) of their lives and present an accumulated picture that reflected key critical points of five individual lives yet remaining coherent in relation to their social and historical contexts. An example from my doctoral thesis given below explains my attempts to make their experiences visible while guarding their personal and professional integrity and the integrity of their voices.

At present, many women like Zehra, Saira, Fatima, Khadija and Rabia, contribute significantly to their families' economies. These women teachers did not just supplement the family income; rather, they were major breadwinners. However, their ability to earn cash income did not significantly improve their position in their families' traditional patterns of gender relations. A dominant position for men in comparison to a submissive one for women still directs the everyday activities of families in the Northern Areas' communities. The five women teachers' experiences offer insights into women's struggle, not only to accomplish their various commitments, but also to change the traditional gender division of tasks. The juxtaposition of their professional lives with their everyday family routines provided a context for each teacher to reflect on gender relationships that had remained indiscernible to others. They found that their families required them to earn money like their male counterparts, yet were not ready to examine the traditional image of womanhood, even in the narrow context of their own household. Rabia and Saira shared their grievances on this issue, because both had male family members with paid jobs. (Ashraf, 2004: 254)

This excerpt is followed by a discussion with quotes and examples from the five women's life histories. This helped me to keep the participants' voices discernable within a collective space. Casey (1993: 25) has used a similar pattern of presenting women teachers' life histories describing it as her attempt to 'create a social space where the collective creators of a discourse can engage in a group conversation'.

Conclusion

This chapter has highlighted the possibilities and challenges of conducting feminist research in the mountainous communities in the Northern Areas of Pakistan. My research experience confirms the possibilities for feminist researchers to conduct research in similar communities elsewhere. However, special consideration is to be given to negotiating the position of the researcher *and* the researched in the indigenous culture that often comprises a complex web of relationship with inherent values and norms. The conventional data collection strategies may also be revisited to examine how these can be contextualized to meet the needs of a specific research context. Finally, self reflexivity, if used well, can allow a feminist researcher to develop insights into how conventional research ethics intersect with the ethics of local indigenous culture during the research process.

In line with the practice of feminist scholarship, the voice and experiences of women were central to my research. In this chapter, the discussions on methodological dimensions of my feminist project are meant to generate its problems from the perspectives of women's experiences, which Harding (1987) considers a distinctive feature of feminist research. By the virtue of this standpoint, I perceive my experiences of conducting a feminist research as an attempt to problemitize the possibilities and challenges of conducting research in my native indigenous culture. The analysis shared earlier revealed that attempts to uphold the feminist principles of visibility of women's voices, reciprocity and elimination of power relationship between researcher and the research participants also had implications for using conventional researching practices. While the discussion suggests possibilities of research, it also recommends a thorough analysis of local cultures in which feminist projects are undertaken.

References

Acker, S., *Gendered Education: Sociological Reflections on Women, Teaching and Feminism* (Toronto, Canada: OISE Press, 1994).

Ashraf, D., 'Experiences of Women Teachers in the Northern Areas of Pakistan', Ph.D. thesis (OISE-UT, Canada, 2004).

Berg, B.L., *Qualitative Research Method for the Social Sciences* (Boston, MA: Allyn and Bacon, 2001).

Bibby, M. (ed.), 'Ethics and Educational Research', *Review of Australian Research in Education*, No 4. (Victoria, Australia: Australian Association for Research in Education, 1997).

Blackmore, J., *Troubling Women: Feminism, Leadership and Educational Change*, (Buckingham, UK: Open University Press, 1999).

Bogdan, R.C., and Biklen, S.K., *Qualitative Research for Education: An Introduction to Theory and Methods*, 3e (New York: Allyn and Bacon, 1998).

Brickhouse, N.W., 'Ethics in Field-based Research: Ethical Principles and Relational Considerations', *Science Education*, 76(1) (1992), 93–103.

Britzman, P.D., *Practice Makes Practice* (New York, NY: State University of New York Press, 1991).

Burgess, R.G., *In Field: An Introduction to Field Research* (London, UK: George Allen and Unwin, 1984).

Casey, K., *I Answer with My Life: Life Histories of Women Teachers Working for Social Change* (New York: Routledge, 1993).

Christians, G.C., 'Ethics and Politics in Qualitative Research', in N.K. Denzin and Y. Lincoln (eds.), *Handbook of Qualitative Research* (New York: Sage, 2000), 135–155.

Creswell, W.J., *Qualitative Inquiry and Research Design: Choosing among Five Traditions* (London, UK: Sage. 1998).

Darlington, Y., and Scott, D., *Qualitative Research in Practice: Stories from the Field* (Buckingham, UK: Open University Press, 2002).

Denzin, N.K., *Interpretive Biography* (Newbury Park, CA: Sage, 1989).

Glesne, C., and Peshkin, A., *Becoming a Qualitative Researcher: An Introduction* (New York: Longman, 1992).

Goodson, I., and Sikes, P., *Life History Research in Educational Settings: Learning from Lives* (Buckingham: Open University Press, 2001).

Haig, B.D., 'Feminist Research Methodology', in J.P. Keeves and G. Lakomski (eds.), *Issues in Educational Research* (Oxford, UK: Pergamon, 1999).

Hall, V., *Dancing on the Ceiling: A Study of Women Managers in Education* (London, UK: Paul Chapman Publishing Ltd, 1996).

Harding, S. (ed.), *Feminism and Methodology: Social Science Issues* (Buckinghamshire, UK: Open University Press, 1987).

Hesse-Biber, N.S., Leavy, P., and Yaiser, L.M., 'Feminist Approaches to Research as a Process: Reconceptualizing Epistemology, Methodology and Method', in N.S. Hesse-Biber and M.L. Yaiser (eds.), *Feminist Perspective on Social Research* (New York: Oxford University Press, 2004), 3–27.

Hesse-Biber, N.S., and Leckenby, D., 'How Feminists Practice Social Research', in N.S. Hesse-Biber and M.L. Yaiser (eds.), *Feminist Perspective on Social Research* (New York: Oxford University Press, 2004), 209–226.

Hesse-Biber, N.S., and Piatelli, D., 'Holistic Reflexivity: The Feminist Practice of Reflexivity', in N.S. Hesse-Biber (ed.), *Handbook of Feminist Research: Theory and Praxis* (Thousand Oaks: Sage Publications, 2007), 493–514.

Hitchcock, G., and Hughes, D., *Research and the Teacher: Qualitative Introduction to School-based Research*, 2e (New York, NY: Routledge, 1995).

Huberman, M., 'Working with Life-history Narrative', in H. McEwan and K. Eagan (eds.), *Narrative in Teaching, Learning, and Research* (New York: Teachers College Press. 1995), 127–165.

Kay, S., 'Writing the Voices of the Less Powerful: Research on Lone Mothers' in J. Ribbens and R. Edwards (eds.), *Feminist Dilemmas in Qualitative Research: Public Knowledge and Private Lives* (London, UK: Sage, 1988).

Maykut, P., and Morehouse, R., *Beginning a Qualitative Research: A Philosophic and Practical Guide* (London, UK: Falmer Press, 1994).

Munro, P., *Subject to Fiction: Women Teachers' Life History Narratives and the Cultural Politics of Resistance* (Buckingham, UK: Open University Press, 1998).

Olesen, L.V., 'Feminism and Qualitative Research at and into the Millennium', in N.K. Denzin and Y.S. Lincoln (eds.), *Handbook of Qualitative Research*, 2e (Thousand Oaks, CA: Sage, 2000), 215–256.

Olesen, V.S., 'Feminism and Qualitative Research at and into the New Millennium', in N. Denzin and Y.S. Lincolns (eds.), *The Landscape of Qualitative Research: Theories and Issues*, 2e (London: Sage Publication, 2003), 332–397.

Plummer, K., *Documents of Life: An Introduction to the Problems and Literature of a Humanistic Method* (London, UK: Allen and Unwin, 1983).

Punch, M., 'Politics and Ethics in Qualitative Research', in N.K. Denzin and Y. Lincoln (eds.), *Handbook of Qualitative Research* (Thousand Oaks, CA: Sage, 1994), 83–97.

Reinharz, S., *Feminist Methods in Social Research* (New York: Oxford University Press, 1992).

Seidman, I., *Interviewing as Qualitative Research: A Guide for Researchers in Education and the Social Sciences*, 2e (New York: Teachers College Press, 1998).

Shah, S., 'The Researcher/interviewer in Intercultural Context: A Social Intruder!', *British Educational Research Journal*, 30(4) (2004), 549–575.

Smith, D.E., 'From Women's Standpoint to a Sociology for People', in J.L. Abu-Lughod (ed.), *Sociology for the Twenty-first Century: Continuities and Cutting Edges* (Chicago, IL: University of Chicago Press, 1999), 65–82.

Sprague, J. and Kobrynowicz, D. 'A Feminist Epistemology', in N.S. Hesse-Biber and M.L. Yaiser (eds.), *Feminist Perspective on Social Research* (New York: Oxford University Press, 2004), 78–100.

Tierney, 'Undaunted Courage: Life History and the Postmodern Challenges', in N.K. Denzin and Y.S. Lincoln (eds.), *Handbook of Qualitative Research*, 2e (Thousand Oaks, CA: Sage, 2000), 537–554.

Weiler, K., *Country School Women: Teaching in Rural California, 1850–1950* (Stanford, CA: Stanford University Press, 1998).

Wilkinson, S., 'Focus Group: A Feminist Method', in N.S. Hesse-Biber and M.L. Yaiser (eds.), *Feminist Perspective on Social Research* (New York: Oxford University Press, 2004), 271–295.

6

The complexity of
researching the lives of
women school leaders in Kenya

JANE F.A. RARIEYA

Introduction

Literature on feminist research abounds with information that seeks to provide clarity on the nature, purposes and processes of conducting feminist qualitative research (Young and Skria, 2003; Jarviluoma, Moisala and Vilkko, 2003; Hesse-Biber and Yaiser, 2004). Whilst these studies may highlight some of the complexities of conducting such research in contexts where there is little or no such research activity, and thereby give the impression that to be forewarned is to be forearmed, the latter is far from the truth.

This chapter seeks to present my experiences of conducting a feminist qualitative study, informed by a critical realist perspective, in the context of a developing country. It aims to contribute to debate and existing literature on the issues and tensions of conducting a feminist study that is qualitative in approach and informed by critical realism. I will begin by discussing the purposes and suitability of adopting a critical realist perspective in studying women in Mombasa, Kenya. This is followed up with a brief discussion of the specific methods employed in the study. In doing so, I will share the methodological and ethical complexities encountered in conducting the study and bring to the fore the issues that arose for me as a researcher both during and at the conclusion of the study. I will also highlight some of the dilemmas I faced as an 'insider', an African woman carrying out research on women in an African context.

The study engaged twelve women who were in educational leadership at the time of the study. The women were heads of either primary or secondary schools and reflected variations in age, marital status, religious affiliations as well as economic status. In particular, I sought to explore how the personal and professional experiences of the women head teachers impacted upon their leadership practices. In doing so, I explored their experiences of becoming and being women and school head teachers. I also sought to investigate whether these experiences were gendered. The foregoing nature of the focus of the study dictated that I employ an approach that would enable me to construct an honest account of school headship based on how the study participants interpreted and 'did' school leadership. Adopting a qualitative paradigm that was informed by a critical realist perspective seemed most amenable for reasons that are discussed in the following sections.

Critical realism as a theoretical foundation for studying women

Critical realism has emerged as a distinct theoretical approach to explain how structures, powers and relations work beneath the observable surface appearance (Archer 2000; Sayer 2000). According to critical realism, the world is not only composed of events, experiences and discourses, but also of underlying structures, powers and tendencies that exist, whether known or not known through experience and/or discourse. This provides the conditions that make it possible for actual events to take place as well as perceived and/or experienced phenomena (Archer 2000). This resonates with my belief that the work we do, how we do it and the perspectives we hold are the products of the interrelationship between our personal biography, our place in the social structure and the cultural setting as well as the historical period in which we live. Hence, in the context of the study, it meant that there were likely to be many influences, experiences and relationships within the head teachers' lives which may have led to them developing a particular philosophy of education and taking on a specific professional identity which informs their work. Furthermore, it was likely that the various contexts and conditions within which head teachers have to work inevitably have an effect upon what they do and how they do it.

In addition, although the underlying levels may possess certain powers and tendencies, these are not always manifested in experience or even for that matter realised. This results in systems and structures that are highly complex and subsequently the possession of powers, potentials, and capacities to act in certain ways, even if those capacities are not realised (Patomaki and Wight 2000). The latter view was particularly pertinent when I set out to commence my study and wondered how the study participants would view their experiences. Furthermore, I wondered whether these experiences were gendered or not.

Thus, critical realism calls for a methodology in which the aim is to explain how social actions and relationships constrain or enable different forms of collective human behaviour (Reed 2005). This is in tandem with my general view of inquiry as an exercise that attempts to know whether or not things are the way they are described, and what it is that makes them appear as such. An inquiry informed by a critical realist perspective would therefore entail methods that are varied and reject universal claims to truth (Denzin and Lincoln, 2005). Such a perspective requires of a researcher to ask what factors must exist in order for human understanding and actions to be patterned in the ways they are observed to be patterned; how do these relations promote or constrain the human freedom and dignity of those involved in them; and therefore, how can they be a resource for those who wish to act to transform the social oppressive structures (Porter, 2003). As a result, it was imperative that my research was one that 'deftly combines historical, structural and discursive analysis to identify and explain the specific causal mechanisms that shape the emergence, elaboration and

transformation of different organizational forms and practices'
(Reed, 2005: 1633).

Adopting a critical realist stance in conducting the study
allowed me, and my participants, to challenge the meanings and
practices that shape their consciousness as women leaders. I,
therefore, viewed critical realism as an approach that would help
me avoid looking at the glass ceilings that women encounter in
school leadership as an obstacle that needs to be penetrated; but
rather, as a phenomenon that needs to be deconstructed to see
what it constitutes as well as seek to understand why and how it
has been maintained (Blackmore, 1998).

Using a critical realist perspective to inform my research study
meant that I had to begin with an in-depth and intensive
historical and structural analysis of pre-existing socio-cultural
practices and contexts. This is because my research question
seemed to imply an explanation which suggested that there is an
underlying truth that is amenable to explanation (Clegg, 2006).
My interest was in the 'underlying enduring deep structures and
mechanisms' (Dobson, 2001: 290) that had resulted in the way
they functioned as leaders. They may have had reasons which
may have been causes of action. However, these reasons had to
be explained in terms of the participants' capacities, their
perceived powers, needs, their situations and contexts as well as
their understanding of all these issues in relation to their
practices as well as the effect of these practices on how school
leadership is subsequently structured (Reed, 2005). Hence, the
study encouraged me as a researcher to look beyond surface
appearances in order to search for the underlying processes that
shape leadership and more specifically, the social relations that
produce, reproduce and transform women's experiences in school
leadership (Archer, 2000). This was especially important because
critical realists do not only engage in discourse analysis but
also identify and challenge sources of oppression (Bhaskar,
1986).

Finally, from the foregoing, it was apparent that I needed to
adopt a research approach that allowed the use of multiple

methods that are interactive 'because the researcher cannot study the whole of 'reality' through one research methodology...' (Jarviluoma, Moisala and Vilkko, 2003: 25). I, too, had realised that one method was not likely to enable me to fully understand the head teachers' experiences and practices. I needed to engage in a number of methods to be able to get a deeper understanding of this. Hence, I employed the use of life history, focus group interviews, observations and documentary evidence.

Negotiating the research terrain

Archer (2000) argues that we have to consider the residual effects of history when we are analysing the social world as we live with structural conditions that we inherit from the past. Since I needed to look into how the historical influences (e.g. the social constructs of leadership as well as the role of women in society and leadership) continue to affect how leadership is practised in Kenya today, I adopted a life history approach. The approach was also suitable because as Goodson and Sikes (2001: 2) aptly argue:

> It [life history] explicitly recognises that lives are not hermetically compartmentalized into, for example, the person we are at work (the professional self) and who we are at home (parent/child/partner/selves), and that, consequently, anything which happens to us in one area of our lives potentially impacts upon and has implications for other areas too; it acknowledges that there is a crucial interactive relationship between individuals' lives, their perceptions and experiences, and historical and social contexts and events; it provides evidence to show how individuals negotiate their identities and consequently, experience, create and make sense of the rules and roles of the social worlds in which they live.

More significant for me as a feminist researcher is that life history is viewed as presenting the research participant in a humanising manner illustrating how history and culture have been lived, thereby enabling the researcher to know the participant as a human individual and ask relevant questions

(McKeown, Clarke and Repper, 2006). Furthermore, it allows for 'a more in-depth exploration of a particular situation, as it generates knowledge characterised by multiple voices, perspectives, truths and meanings' (Kakuru and Paradza, 2007: 288). Finally, feminist research advocates research processes and outcomes that are beneficial to the research participant (see Rhode, 2003; Hesser-Biber andYaiser, 2004) and indeed, life history does so as it provides the participants opportunities to tell their stories in their own words and thereby benefit from the empathy and audience presented by the researcher (Kakuru and Paradza, 2007). This approach, therefore, provided me with individual head teacher's life story that enabled me not only to explore each head teacher's background, in order to develop an understanding of how they arrived at leadership, but also their experiences which are a source of the way they practice leadership today (Curry, 1997). I also used this approach to understand the source of their interpretations of how they viewed themselves as leaders. It helped me to construct how various social contexts were played out in the lives of individual head teachers as well as to get a feeling for how things were before I began my relationship with them in this study (Wolcott, 1997). However, these very attributes of methodology were the ones that I found problematic as discussed later in the chapter.

In addition, I used observations. Sometimes, I would turn up for interviews and find the participants in meetings, teaching, some supervision activity and so forth. In these situations, I would retreat into observing the participants as I waited for them to finish whatever they were doing. These observation opportunities allowed me to see how the head teachers interacted with other people and enacted their role as head teachers. They also enabled me to find out some more things about the participants but in as much as they provided me with data that helped to fill gaps, in some instances, they presented ethical dilemmas, especially in instances when I found out things that I thought the participant may not have wanted me to know.

I also used focus group interviews and documentary evidence. I was of the view that the context in which the head teacher worked and observation of their workplace dictated the use of the aforementioned methods. The use of these qualitative data collection methods presented me with certain complexities which I present in later sections of this chapter.

Entering the field

The first complexity I encountered was with regard to gaining entry into the field to conduct my study. This stage was wrought with complexities which were mainly due to the research, particularly of the nature I proposed to do (an in-depth 'intrusive' study), which was not common in this context. I was cognizant of the discomfort that was likely to arise if I asserted that I was doing a gender study because the advent of feminism in Kenya in the late 1970s was clearly feared. It can be argued that a modified version of that fear is still present in the Kenyan society where feminists are sometimes perceived as challenging 'natural' differences between men and women. In addition, I was aware that researchers who are outsiders are often treated with suspicion; I had thought that because I was more or less a local, since I had resided and taught in the district for a number of years in the past, my 'insider' position would lessen this suspicion. This was not to be: my 'insider-outsider' status only served to complicate matters in many instances as discussed below. As a researcher trained at a university in the North, I had arrived in this research setting with certain preconceived ideas. However, I was forced to reconsider the assumptions I had made based on a well-prepared and rehearsed 'How to do' list.

The experiences I encountered in trying to gain entry into the schools varied and were dependent on whether the school was private or public (government). Prior to formally inviting the head teacher to take part in the study, I decided to pay a visit to a number of schools headed by female head teachers and talk to them about my intended study. This was crucial, because as stated earlier, in this context, research is viewed with suspicion and researchers are seen as people who come to unearth unsavoury details of the school which may later find their way into the local newspapers. After all, the research that most people are familiar with in this context is that of investigative journalism. In addition, as stated earlier, gender-related issues tend to elicit mixed feelings; therefore, it was important for me to get a feel of how my research was likely to be received.

Talking with a few head teachers enabled me to assess the general reaction to my study and also determine how many head teachers were willing to participate in the study. I was in a difficult situation of wanting to both sell *and* not sell the study. It felt somewhat paradoxical to, on the one hand, be asserting the worth of a project focusing on women head teachers' lives, and at the same time insisting that no one should feel obliged to participate. However, I knew that the methods intended to employ in the study would enable me to work on these issues. I, then, proceeded to a more formal request to engage them in my study. Whilst I did identify the schools whose heads I wanted to study, in the end, the final decision rested with the school management board in the case of private schools, and the Ministry of Education for the government schools.

In the case of private schools, I wrote to either the school board, school committee or owner (as was applicable) seeking permission to conduct my study in their schools. Whilst most of the head teachers in the primary schools were thrilled at the prospect of taking part in the study and no doubt 'pushed' their employers to let them take part in the study, the same could not be said of their secondary school counterparts. I was not surprised by the enthusiasm displayed by the former as I have often found the primary school environment in Kenya to be warm and welcoming, always drawing me into it, in comparison to that of the secondary school. Most of the private secondary schools that I approached had head teachers of Asian origin and they declined to take part in the study. Interestingly, the head teachers of Asian origin in the primary schools also declined to take part in the study. I could only surmise that the Asian community in

Mombasa was still a closed one (Naipaul, 1980) and did not relish the thought of someone 'poking around in their backyard'. The result was that in the secondary schools category, I had more head teachers from the government schools than the private schools, although at the outset, I had hoped to have an equal number in both categories.

In the case of the government schools, I had to travel to the Ministry of Education Headquarters in Nairobi (about 500 kilometres away from Mombasa) to seek permission, as is the policy, to get into government schools as well as to present myself for an interview about my intentions and the intended outcome of my study. Thereafter, a high ranking education ministry official gave me a letter granting me permission to enter specific schools for purposes of conducting my study. I later submitted copies of this letter of authorisation to the Municipal Education Office (for the primary schools) and the District Education Office (for the secondary schools) for endorsement to access the said schools. At both these offices, I had to re-explain what I wanted to do in the schools despite having attached what I thought were lucid self-explanatory letters. It was at this level that my selection of schools was changed either because the heads were on transfer or due to retire during the period of data collection. In one instance, one of the head teachers was dropped from my list because the education office did not perceive her to be a 'model' female head of school. As a result, a dilemma arose out of this collaboration with the Education Ministry in gaining entry into schools. On one hand, the ministry's approval served as a gate opener to gaining unlimited entry into the schools. On the other, it caused resentment amongst some of the head teachers as they ended up being participants in a study for which their personal permission had not been sought. This was further compounded by the fact that they could not refuse to participate because it would have been equated to defying instructions given by a superior at the workplace. As this seemed part of the usual formalities and protocols of gaining entry into the field, it seemed appropriate for me to go along with this and then to make a point of discussing the issues of voluntary consent in more detail with the participants at the start of actual data collection. This, I believed, would allow them to find out more about the study, its aims and objectives, and key research questions, as well as the commitments and expectations on the part of the researcher and themselves as participants.

Data gathering

Another level of complexity arose during the actual data collection period. My choice of data collection methods was based on the assumption that the concept of leadership based on personal and professional experiences is both contextualised and relational and would have to be investigated by various means. As a result, I decided to conduct interviews of both the head teachers (primary participants) and teachers and students (secondary participants); conduct observations of the head teachers in their school settings; read documents as well as engage in informal conversations with the participants and others in the research setting.

I found that interviewing the women head teachers was a quagmire of complexities. Prior to the commencement of the study, a few had seemed very enthusiastic about being participants in the study and all of them had seemed willing to be interviewed. On the whole, they were polite and though clearly busy, they made an effort to create time to be interviewed. However, some of the participants with whom I had had previous interactions— I had either taught their children or they had been my colleagues in the past- seemed to be the most difficult to work with. I repeatedly found that seeking them out for an interview was a constant mind game and power play at work. I did not know whether this attitude was born out of being familiar with me or their discomfort at the likelihood of my finding out some 'unsavoury' aspects of their lives or practices. This left me feeling frustrated and put out but determined to go on because dropping them might have necessitated a trip back to the Provincial Director of Education's Office to seek alternate participants.

This would have boomeranged on me: not only would it have brought out these head teachers in a bad light with their superiors and possibly led to some disciplinary action, but also, it would have galvanised the rest of the head teachers in sympathising with them, leading to a possible subtle rejection of my study and I. After all, I was the 'outsider.'

Life history interviews usually begin by giving the research participant an opportunity to tell their life story, which is viewed as an empowering approach. However, in telling their stories the participant may fail to talk about areas that the researcher may consider important to the study. To mitigate this, I used an interview schedule to guide the interviews.

As mentioned earlier, I also engaged in non-participant observation which Wolcott (1999: 48) describes as the kind of observation where 'researchers make no effort to hide what they are doing or to deny their presence, but neither are they able fully to avail themselves of the potential afforded by participant observation to take a more active or interactive role'. However, my role as an observer ranged from being an 'observer-visitor' to 'passive observer' (Wolcott, 1999: 336) depending on whether the observations were obtrusive or unobtrusive. Since everyone in the school was aware that I was working with the head teacher, I was generally seen as the head teacher's 'person', and because of the power that surrounds the person of the head of school, I kept as low a profile as possible because I was anxious not to be regarded as an evaluator of what everybody was doing in the school, and someone who was likely to report back to the head teacher.

During the data collection period, I was made keenly aware of how an otherwise 'innocuous' equipment can complicate matters in the field. At that time, the press in Kenya was awash with revelations by a former senior government official of indicting tape recordings that he had made of senior cabinet members without their knowledge. So participants were particularly uneasy and constantly referred to my tape recorder asking for assurance that their words would not come to haunt them in a similar fashion as the cabinet ministers. As a result, there were often requests to switch off the tape recorder, which sometimes meant that I was unable to record what I considered vital information. I had to quickly learn to develop a form of shorthand in order to enable me to write down the interview, an activity I found rather arduous as these interviews were quite lengthy, an hour or so.

Relationships in the field

The study also illustrated the complexity that surrounds relationships between the researcher and the researched in this context, which may not necessarily preclude other settings (see Chapter 5). As this was a study that was intruding in the participants' lives, in fact dealing with some sensitive and intimate matters in their lives, several ethical issues arose during the study which I will discuss in the ensuing section.

First and foremost, my positionality within the research process played an important role in the development of the nature of relationships between me, the researcher, and my research participants, i.e., individual head teachers. Although I am a Kenyan woman who was researching Kenyan women, I found that my own identity as a Kenyan was not enough to develop reciprocal relationships and understandings with my participants. As stated earlier, though I did not consider myself an outsider to the culture in which this study took place—I was Kenyan, had taught for a number of years in Mombasa and had been in educational management—for various reasons I was perceived very much as an outsider. This was probably because I no longer worked in Mombasa or even Kenya for that matter. Working in other contexts had indeed resulted in my acquiring certain habits that may not have been considered Kenyan. In addition, there were times when I did not look at issues using a 'Kenyan' lens. On the other hand, I was largely acceptable to the head teachers because I had been a teacher, and indeed a well-known teacher in Mombasa for many years, a deputy head teacher, and had been involved in the management of schools of a particularly well-known school system. Nonetheless, I was aware that I would need to work hard to gain the participants' trust and confidence for them to dedicate time to the interviews and to speak frankly about personal and professional issues with me.

Secondly, I saw my experiences as a woman as well as proximity in age to some of the head teachers in the study as central to my role as a researcher in this context. In a way, my sex and its possibly related gender issues contributed to my acceptability by the participants for it was assumed that I would be able to understand their experiences because of this.

Thirdly, based on my experiences in researching and teaching gender issues in Pakistan, I had anticipated that the women heads may be reluctant to discuss gender issues. This necessitated the establishment of trust between the head teacher and me as well as the teachers, students and me. Right from the start, I accepted that I could not be impassive if I wanted to get them to open up: I too had to open up. Oakley (1981: 49) aptly points out that there is 'no intimacy without reciprocity'. I, therefore, drew upon the parallels between the head teacher's personal and professional experiences and mine. Pointing these parallels facilitated in gradually developing rapport with my research participants.

I also found that interviewing the head teachers was a 'contradiction in terms' (Oakley, 1981: 46). The extent to which the participants were forthcoming with information varied between individuals. For example, at the start of the study, some of the head teachers seemed a little reserved and suspicious of what I was up to. It was difficult to even get some of them to consent to the first interview despite having agreed to take part in the study. I felt that perhaps they were not too sure how much the study would delve into their lives, and possibly the follies that lay therein. It was probable, too that that the initial response of some of them during the interviews was because, as stated earlier, I had been 'imposed' on them. At first I was alarmed by the subtle tensions between us. However, I quickly came to understand that the tensions and a lack of positive understanding between us provided me with an alternative perspective of them as school leaders than an overly mutually accommodating relationship may have.

Although one of the recognised advantages of life history is that it gives research participants a voice and enables the researcher to hear this voice (Downie & Cottrell, 2001), one must acknowledge that the researcher is more powerful than the participants. After all, the research questions, choice of participants, how the participants respond to given questions, and the analysis of their responses are all affected by the researcher's identity and characteristics (Kakuru and Paradza, 2007). Therefore, while I was cognizant of the fact that as a woman academic who was also pursuing her doctoral degree at a university in the North, I wielded some power and authority which was likely to intimidate or make the participants uncomfortable, I found that some of the participants attempted to exercise their power over me. For example, I found that those heads who were particularly difficult at the start of the study attempted to lord their power over me to claim their authority and control over the research process. These power dynamics between the participants and myself affected the nature of our relationships in the field throughout the study.

In addition, I found myself querying as to what extent the participants should be probed, especially, when they seemed reluctant to talk about events in their lives which I was aware of, as an insider, having had an impact on their lives. For example, one of the head teachers had in the past been transferred when she was a teacher because of differences between her and the then principal. Although I was aware of the incident, I was of the view that I would get to hear the participant's side of the story. However, this was not forthcoming despite my hunches that the way she related to her teachers was partly a result of this incident. I did not know whether to probe until what I understood to be a significant aspect of her life was revealed or whether to respect her right to decide what information to share and accept that the participants are under no obligation to tell all to the researcher.

Furthermore, there were many sad things that happened in the schools that made me emotional and I realised that it was impossible to demarcate my role as a researcher from my role as a human being (Oakley, 1981). For instance, I recall walking into one of the schools and finding the head teacher and a few teachers clustered together, talking in whispers and looking very anxious. I then found out that one of the pupils, a six-year old girl, had been abducted and raped. As a result, I was unable to conduct any interviews on that day as both the head teacher and the teachers were busy trying to calm down anxious students and parents. On another occasion, I remember feeling both angry and sad when, during an interview, one of the students told me that she preferred to stay in school as late as she could because she found it safe and there she was not likely to be abused by her stepfather as usually happened at home.

Ethical issues

As a doctoral student at a British university, I sought to adhere to the BERA code of ethical and professional conduct for research as well as keep in mind a list of ethical issues (Miles and Huberman, 1994: 290–7) that typically need attention before, during and after qualitative studies.

Although, I endeavoured to make the study as ethical as possible, there were several issues that arose in the field that made me wonder how ethical one could really be when conducting a qualitative study and a feminist one at that, especially in the context where the study took place. I found myself faced with ethical issues that could not easily be traced in books. I became profoundly aware of how ethical issues, although important to address explicitly at the commencement of a study, are of ongoing significance to a process-oriented study like the one I was engaged in. I quickly realized that a researcher has to see ethical issues as more than an administrative detail and instead be very concerned about the issues he or she would need to consider prior to, during and after the study.

Prior to collecting data, I discussed the purpose and procedures of the study with the participants so that they could anticipate what to expect during the research process. I, therefore, got informed consent from them by getting them to append their signatures to explanatory letters which clearly and accurately disclosed the purpose of the study, methods of collecting data and made a provision of allowing the participants to withdraw any time they felt uncomfortable with the process or the ideas under discussion. Although participants were informed that their participation was voluntary and that they could withdraw any time, I wondered how voluntary the participation of some of the head teachers of government schools really was. The bureaucratic nature of getting into such schools to conduct research, which I described earlier, did not allow the head teachers the freedom to outrightly decline to participate, whatever their reasons may have been. In fact, declining to participate was tantamount to insubordination as the signature on the official letter permitting the researcher to enter a particular school was from a very high ranking ministry official. So, while on the surface signing a consent letter seemed a good basis from which to start our work, I found that it inadvertently compromised rapport between me and the participants in the initial stages of data collection. Also, a number of the head teachers were uneasy about signing the letters. In the context of Kenya, appending signatures to a document is a very serious action that merits wide consultation. Also, by requiring the participants' signatures, the consent letter took a formal tone that transcended into the first interviews; I had to work hard to break down the formality so that the participants could relax, talk with ease and not tell me things they thought I wanted to hear.

In addition, the consent letters assured the participants of the protection of their identity. However, I found that it was difficult to do this in the field. By going through the education office to seek permission to go into the government schools, which my participants were, was public knowledge. Quite often, I felt embarrassed when upon completing an interview and packing up to leave, one head teacher would ask me if I had been to see so and so. Also, other head teachers would call me up and wonder why I had not asked them to participate in the study and yet saw it fit to take on so and so. All these queries served to remind me that I needed to be extra careful in the write-up of the findings so that nothing could be traced back to the individual head teacher. In doing so, I believed I would be protecting their identities and, therefore, protecting them from harm both socially or professionally.

In the students' case, I sought consent from their parents or guardians through the head teacher. However, in some schools, the head teachers took it upon themselves to sign the forms on behalf of the parents as they felt that the parents would either not bother or were not literate; they assured me that should there be any consequences, they would take full responsibility for them. Such parental response is typical of the Kenyan context where parents believe that when they take their children to school, the school is solely responsible for their children. It is expected, though this expectation is hardly voiced aloud, that whatever the decision the school makes on behalf of their children is often for the latter's good. No doubt, there have been occasions when this trust has been abused.

I was also obliged to promise the participants that there would be no harm to them as a result of participating in this research; I was rather reluctant to enter into this kind of agreement with them. This was because I felt that the nature of this particular study was such that the participants might be made to reveal certain personal characteristics or information that may make them uncomfortable and in some cases, the in-depth interviewing may force them to face aspects about themselves that they normally do not consider and this may provoke adverse reactions. Indeed, several times, the participants either broke down and cried or banged tables in anger as they recalled profound incidents in their lives. Although I always gave them the option of not answering a question if they found it too intrusive, none of the heads declined to answer any question, despite the 'emotional storms' that brewed up during some of the interviews.

Kakuru and Paradza (2007) describe how participants in their study in Uganda and Zimbabwe readily discussed their stories because they anticipated some assistance. Likewise, in interviewing teachers, I was constantly dogged by requests for lunch or a soda (soft drink) and a snack. These requests would come from the head teacher or their deputies. At first, I resisted these requests because I was of the opinion that it would seem like I was buying information, which is unethical according to the international guidelines, and explained the same to the head teacher or their deputies. However, as these requests became persistent and when it became difficult to get teachers together for the group interviews, I bowed to pressure and ensured that the teachers were served with lunch or soda depending on the time of the interview. I was amazed at how swiftly teachers were able to come together for interviews once they were informed that I would provide some refreshment. There were requests for financial payment for accepting to take part in the interviews, which I firmly declined and informed the head teacher and deputies that it was not necessary for such people to be part of the group interview. This made me realise that where poverty is prevalent and people barely meet their basic needs, almost everything is up for sale. In other contexts, especially in the North, once people are assured of protection from any harm as a result of the study, they are generally willing to participate for the sake of contributing to the generation and dissemination of knowledge for the common good; it was difficult to expect all participants to take part in the study for this purpose.

With all the ethical issues that arose in the field, I found myself taking the view propagated by Christians (2005), who reflects that 'the code of ethics should serve as a guideline prior to fieldwork but not intrude on full participation' (Punch, 1944: 144). The strict application of the code of ethics that was developed in the North was likely to interfere with what was an otherwise inoffensive study in the context of a developing country.

Value of the research

Whilst adopting a critical realist perspective, undertaking this study enabled me to engage in a historical, structural and discursive analysis of factors that contributed to the manifestation of school leadership as portrayed by the head teachers in the study. I left the field feeling uncomfortable. The reflexive nature of the study ensured the head teachers to think more reflectively of their experiences and the relation between their experiences and their leadership practices. Many found themselves questioning existing systems that had marginalised and continue to marginalise the head teachers and women in general in Kenya. Others found themselves questioning their leadership practices. However, I found myself haunted by strong feelings that this study did not deal with the resultant dissonance that it may have caused the participants. It was not a participatory study that would have mobilised the head teachers to act. As a result, I found myself asking questions about the purpose of doing such a study in a context like Kenya where much help and effort is needed to eradicate dominant prevailing gender inequalities in education and people need to be mobilised to act in order to improve social conditions.

Conclusion

This chapter has in a way highlighted the political nature of conducting a feminist qualitative study that is informed by critical realism. Hence, it can be seen that whilst the research activities were informative and provided me with numerous moments for learning, the research process as a whole brought its own methodological challenges. It is evident that engaging in this kind of a research is framed by certain socio-political arrangements that may be peculiar to the specific context(s) in which it is being conducted. My experiences have demonstrated that in as much as such qualitative research has particular universal features that determine its nature and purposes, the processes are very much context dependent, thereby making it more complex than the standard 'how to' guides reveal.

References

Archer, M.S., *Being Human: The Problem of Agency* (Cambridge: Cambridge University Press, 2002).

Bhaskar, R., *Scientific Realism and Human Emancipation* (London: Verso, 1986).

Blackmore, J., 'Educational Leadership: A Feminist Critique and Reconstruction', in J. Smyth (ed.), *Critical Perspectives in Educational Leadership* (New York: Falmer Press, 1998), 99–131.

Christians, C.G., 'Ethics and Politics in Qualitative Research', in N.K. Denzin and Y.S. Lincoln (eds.), *The Sage Handbook of Qualitative Research*, 3e (Thousand Oaks, CA: Sage, 2005), 139–164.

Clegg, S., 'The Problem of Agency in Feminism: A Critical Realist Approach', *Gender and Education*, 18 (3) (2006), 309–324.

Curry, B.K., 'The Life Experiences of Women and their Leadership Practice', *International Studies in Educational Administration*, 25 (2) (1997), 106–114.

Denzin, N.K., and Lincoln, Y.S., 'The Discipline and Practice of Qualitative Research', in N.K. Denzin and Y.S. Lincoln (eds.), *The Sage Handbook of Qualitative Research*, 3e (Thousand Oaks, CA: Sage, 2005), 1–32.

Dobson, P.J., 'Longitudinal Case Research: A Critical Realist Perspective', *Systemic Practice and Action Research*, 14 (3) (2001), 283–296.

Downie, J., and Cottrell, B., 'Community-based Research Ethics Review: Reflections on Experiences and Recommendations for Action', *Health Law Review*, 19 (1) (2001), 8–18.

Goodson I., and Sikes P., *Life History Research in Educational Settings: Learning from Lives* (Buckingham: Open University Press, 2001).

Hesse-Biber, S.N., and Yaiser, M.L. (eds.), *Feminist Perspectives on Social Research* (Oxford: Oxford University Press, 2004).

Jarviluoma, H., Moisala, P., and Vilkko, A., *Gender and Qualitative Methods* (London: Sage, 2003).

Kakuru, D.M., and Paradza, G.G., 'Reflections on the use of the Life History Method in Researching Rural African Women: Field Experiences from Uganda and Zimbabwe', *Gender and Development*, 15 (2) (2007), 287–297.

Mckeown, J., Clarke, A., and Repper, J., 'Life Story Work in Health and Social Care: Systematic Literature Review', *Journal of Advanced Nursing*, 55 (2) (2006), 237–247.

Miles, M.B., and Huberman, A.M., *Qualitative Data Analysis*, 2e (Thousand Oaks, CA: Sage, 1994).

Naipaul, S., *North of South: African Journey* (London: Penguin, 1980).

Oakley, A., 'Interviewing Women', in H. Roberts (ed.), *Doing Feminist Research* (New York: Routledge & Kegan Paul, 1981), 30–61.

Patomaki, H., and Wight C., 'After Postpositivism? The Promises of Critical Realism', *International Studies Quarterly*, 44 (2000), 213–237.

Porter, S., 'Realism', in R.L. Miller and J.D. Brewer (eds.), *The A–Z of Social Research* (London: Sage, 2003), 256–259.

Reed, M., 'Reflections on the "Realist Turn" in Organization and Management Studies', *Journal of Management Studies*, 42(8) (2005), 1621–1644.

Rhode, D.L. (ed.), *The Difference 'Difference' Makes: Women and Leadership* (Stanford, CA: Stanford University Press, 2003).

Sayer, A., *Realism and Social Science* (London: Sage, 2000).

Wolcott, H.F., 'Ethnographic Research in Education', in R.M. Jaeger (ed.), *Methods for Research in Education*, 2e (Washington, DC: American Educational Research Association, 1997), 327–353.

Wolcott, H.F., *Ethnography: A Way of Seeing* (Oxford: Altamira Press, 1999).

Young, M.D., and Skrla, L. (eds.), *Reconsidering Feminist in Educational Leadership* (Albany, NY: State University of New York Press, 2003).

7

Experience and identity

The ethnographer as a practising artist

MEHRI HONARBIN-HOLLIDAY

Introduction

This paper stems from a doctoral study of the development of art education in the Islamic Republic of Iran at the Visual Arts Departments at Tehran University and Al-Zahra University for Women, and the interrelationships between art training in theory and practice and the concept of identity. In light of the increasing discussions and reflections by scholars positioning and viewing social phenomena within interdisciplinary perspectives, this study might be considered a milestone in the evolutionary path of interdisciplinarity in qualitative research. In this instance the boundaries of enquiry in education, sociology and art are softened as the participants' personal histories and experiences are related and the site of the research is expanded to include the researcher's studio in Canterbury. The production of art objects by the researcher are thus given parity and equal weight as other data within the work, especially as they are reflections of the participants' shared and common experiences and heritage. This has ultimately meant that the theoretical tools adopted in the field in Tehran are also applied to the researcher, who is of Iranian birth and educated in Britain, in order to better understand the field and determine her location in the enquiry.

With regard to time and place, three extended visits were made to the primary site of the enquiry in Tehran over a period of six months, between January and December 2002. These visits were made to observe the 2D and 3D 'practice and theory' at the two campuses, the Faculty of Art and Architecture at Tehran University and the Applied Arts Department at Al-Zahra University for Women. The participants were undergraduate students, key lecturers, and tutors. Several lecturers and tutors had been recently trained in France on government scholarships and were politically affiliated with the Islamic regime. Several from this group were also members of the Academic Council or 'Hay-at-e elmi' with direct power and input into the selection of the heads of departments and new faculty/staff. There were also a number of participants who were sessional tutors without any political affiliations, but popular amongst the student body because of their expertise in both theory and practice of art. The observations and interviews to establish curriculum and staffing structures that had developed since the 1979 Revolution, involved both students and key scholars in the two campuses. As a result of these enquiries, however, the field of study broadened, and there emerged a chain of interconnected locations such as the private atelier system where most sessional tutors hold private classes, and the Tehran Museum of Contemporary Art as the site for public cultural exchange and cultural dialogue.

The exchange of ideas and art discourses, including reflections about the meaning of private and public art in Muslim majority Iran, thus travelled from one space or institution to another with an overall quality comparable to discourses of art worldwide. This was with the exception of nudity and erotic arts which are categorically banned in the Islamic Republic as they are in many countries in the East and West. Since late 2005 however, and interrelated to the hardline policies associated with the 2005 presidential elections and its outcomes, Tehran Museum of Contemporary Art has distanced itself from the forward looking and ground breaking liberal programmes and pursued the attitudes prevalent between 1997 and 2005. The atelier system continues to function as a more liberal space for artistic practice and expression with an output of diverse art works which continue to arrive in numerous major galleries in major cities in the West.

The choice of adopting the qualitative paradigm allowed for fluidity in gathering data, and facilitated both the illumination, and examination of the building blocks of the history and the architecture in the development of art education in Iran since 1979, rather than a system of counting those building blocks and arriving at quantitative numerical arrangements of charts, graphs, and percentages. The methods and means of gathering data varied according to the sensibilities and circumstances at the research site.

Having reflected on the ethical aspect of the project, it was agreed with the participants in Tehran, both campuses, that direct quotations from interviews could be used in the thesis. This in turn led to a diverse collection of personal views and histories relating to perceptions about art training and forms in ideological expression and political trajectories. Structured and semi-structured recorded interviews, recorded conversations, observational notes on what was said and shown to the researcher, photographs, and other visual material enriched the interviews. There emerged bodies of ideas and lived experiences which indicated multiple and complex individual identities. The clay sculptures executed by the researcher in response to the notion of reflexivity, identity, and experience, and her visual diary, self-ethnography using a hand held digital video camera, gathered significance as the research progressed. Both the clay sculptures, and the visual diary in the form of an art video were shipped to Iran to be viewed by the participants. The thesis, thus culminated in the production and management of a range of ideas and perceptions in written, sculptural, and visual texts, illuminating the interconnections between art and identities.

In the following paragraphs I shall reflect on the continuum of theories and practices employed as my conceptual framework to access and process deeper understanding of ontologies in Tehran. I shall analyse the nucleus of reflexive and critical ethnographic texts also with regard to the Derridean concept of deconstruction and différance in order to indicate histories, perspectives, and layers in epistemologies from the field. I shall create intersections between those ethnographies and Clifford Geertz's notion of 'text' as a facility for communicating meaning. I shall further engage with the suggestion that 'texts' can be written or visual as they are constructed and given, or created by the participants with the intention to communicate particular and significant meanings. I shall maintain the perception that ethnographic texts cannot be limited to their literary form, but may be oral, visual, and sculptural. I shall further propose that positioning and juxtapositioning such texts, as if in a map possessing contours, will reveal the embedded qualities in perceptions, ideologies, and complex identities.

Critical and reflexive ethnographies

I have selected the ethnographic method because of its dynamic approach to social scientific research where perceptions about humans are formed through systematically observing their behaviours and listening to the accounts of their lived experience and perceptions. This method is dynamic because of the range of observational tools available to the ethnographer; watching, listening, making notes, interacting, photography, and making videos are increasingly employed on the ethnographic path to deconstruct, record, register, reveal, and document human condition and experience.

My focus, however, has been on critical and reflexive developments in such ethnographic observations, where normative and universal claims to hermeneutics and truths are critiqued by the participants (Carspecken, 1996). This gives credence to the diverse views and realities expressed by those being observed, placing attention on the diversities in perceptions and multi-layered meanings in a globalized world. Related to critical theory, reflexive and critical ethnography gain ground from cultural criticism. This is where the complex and multiple nature of politics and identities, and the notion of participation in cultural discourses might be pursued and examined with the consideration of class, ethnicity, and gender. Related to origins as varied as the critical traditions of Marx, the Chicago School of Sociology, the Frankfurt School, feminist ideology and methodologies, and the post-structuralism of Michel Foucault and Jacques Derrida, these approaches contemplate and scrutinize the notions of power, liberation, and resistance while observing phenomena (Ladson-Billings, 2000; Kincheloe and McLaren, 2000; Lincoln and Guba, 2000; Tedlock, 2000).

I have thus become especially alerted to the specificities in the lived experience of the participants in Tehran and the political and cultural issues raised as the result of their reflexive and critical data. The extract from an interview with a male student from Tehran University whose lectures I was observing makes a good example. This interviewee chose not to respond directly to my specific questions about the quality of teaching and learning processes during the period of observation, and instead addressed a chain of relationships which were at once about art and culture and geopolitics. In his discussion he provides insights beyond the university campus where he studies art, and into the nature and dominance of Western hegemony even through art. He stated the following:

I know that you were expecting a discussion about my work as a graduating painter/sculptor, and the metaphysical thought in Henri Matisse's work, which I am discussing in my dissertation. But I have decided to make a statement about the state of the world. I want to tell you that I, the air I breathe, the milk I drink, this university, our government, and many governments like it around the globe are enslaved by the power systems in the West. The American greed, its Zionist chain of control and capitalism, have crippled us. This is what we talk about at home in the evenings when there is nothing on television to watch, when we are tired of our books, when we see images of war on our televisions, all kinds of war, and when there cannot be any trust in anyone who has anything to do with power. Tell me, don't they look around themselves, and think in the West? Did you know that Clinton has already been to countries north of the Caspian Sea and secured all rights for the future pipelines and the gas in the region? The gas which is still deep underground and not yet been decided for, or its extent fully clarified by the indigenous people in that region? So we think what is the use of this industry?

You mentioned 'autonomy and art'. Let me tell you about your celebrity ridden autonomous art, your worship of anything that is driven by money. When Christo wraps mountains in cloth, like a record in its sleeve, when he covers a skyscraper in Berlin and stands on top of it to be worshiped as 'the object' in space, he is ruled by capitalism, and the money it depends on. Just think about the sponsors.... Money, our money, the oil money, the money we cannot have. The money we need to spend on a thousand and one things to improve lives here, and to secure futures here. So, of what significance would my few canvases and sculptures be in the dirty scale of things. If you want to interview me, consider these issues, what other chance do I have to speak to that world of yours?

This reflexive and critical response alerted me to reflect and consider how the condition of the locale might be and often is examined in relation to the global systems of power. Here it happens to be put forth by a Tehran University student. His analysis and viewpoint are widespread in Iran as well as the Middle East. Inspite of the uncertainties, the young man expresses his own future, his doubtful employment prospects in governmental institutions because of his lack of support for the strict religiosity expected of him, he further proposes the region's position in relation to the bigger picture in geopolitics, implicating the oil hungry West. This in turn directly reflects on the U.S.'s foreign and monetary policies because of the oil resources in the region on the one hand, and on the other, how the grandiose and dependency of significant works of art on the capitalist machinery. Thus, an art student in Tehran considers the works of artists such as the renowned Bulgarian-born American installation artist Christo Vladimirov Javacheff to be hegemonic because the costly large scale projects which are often several miles long are probably executed with the financial backing of conglomerates whose money could very easily be sourced from his region.

Similarly, adopting such theoretical tools facilitated the fluid and layered reconstruction and presentation of the voice of the female participants both individually and collectively. Rather than observing just the teaching and learning processes between students and tutors, critical and reflexive ethnographies emboldened the researcher to value and include a wider range of experiences embedded in the data. As a result, a space for gendered identities emerged where ethnographic texts were culminated in relating the women's sense of agency in authoring and structuring their lives as individuals and citizens. The texts illuminated forms of resistance and broader critical perspectives in Iranian society. The following are examples given by two art students. The first relates nuances in Islamic identity which can be directly integral to individual identities and personal goals, neither of which is perceived in conjunction with familial or societal limitations. And the second relates diversity in perception often not associated with women in the Muslim world.

The following is Maryam's statement giving insights into her life world:

I am from a political-religious family, and I am a supporter of the Iranian government and its stance on theologies; this is after all due to the revolution of the minorities. My family did not think studying art was suitable for me because one or two of my cousins, sadly, lost all sense of their roots when they went to university to study art. I married at 15 and now have a 12 year old son. I have, however, taken advantage of adult education courses and the Educational *Jahad*[1] to make up for the lost years to pursue my interests in art. I investigated a number of universities including Al-Zahra which I found unappealing due to the student body being all female. It became clear that I wanted to study at Tehran University. I was assisted in all these by the '*jahad-e danesh-gahi*'. I did a foundation course there and was taught art history to help me prepare for the university entrance examination. I also attended Mr Arkhas' classes for drawing, but I was put off by everyone becoming a little like him. He seemed very single minded.

I could not have achieved all this without my husband's support and constant encouragement. I get home when I get home in the evenings, sometimes at 9 o'clock. Whoever gets there first, cooks. Raising our son is taken seriously by both my husband and myself, but my work is suffering at the moment, it is naïve of women to want it all and have it all. Terms such as 'liberated' and 'free' are difficult statements, I am trying to reach my goal. I have a set of aims. I hope to go abroad, Germany where I have relatives, to familiarise myself with other ways of looking at art. I believe they are much more 'scientific' in their approach. As the Prophet has said learning is a duty even if it is to be sought in far away China. I think it would feed into my own work, and perhaps, I might be able to teach it.

Whilst this text provides multiple meanings that tell of Maryam's ability to manage well, the most notable are, in my view, the ways in which she has imagined a future for herself, has located a set of personal goals, and has set out to shape her life in order to achieve those goals. She further reveals that she will not be stereotyped because of her religious beliefs and attend a university specifically for women. Rather she has made a choice and is determined to go to the university which has a mixed student body where she could benefit from interacting with the opposite sex.

Anahita, a student from Al-Zahra University for Women, has made the following contribution:

Yes I like to paint images of my own body, sometimes without clothes. Well it is only a body and we all have it, don't we? My body, your body, it is a common language that's all. I don't know what it means to paint 'beautiful' things, is something beautiful when you can't take your eyes off it? I paint the bathroom too, I have just painted my head in the middle of the space in the bathroom. At the moment I stack my paintings under my bed. A friend and I are looking for a space, a studio, somewhere near college so we can make big canvases. It is difficult though, most houses want to let rooms to tidy people and we want to spill paint everywhere.

A third year painting student, Anahita puts forth her reflexive views and ideas through her paintings and the complex and universal language of art. Indeed she addresses her critique through the language of the body. While her painting cannot be presented to us physically to view here, we might consider what she means through an analysis of her suggestion of the language of the body. This language culminates in the capabilities and power of the body as a tool and concept: a warm and shaped object moving in space, able to at once articulate that space by its presence and dominate it with gestures. The potential of the formal qualities of the body has been the big idea in art since Classicism. The body is suggestive of numerous perspectives, including power, solidity, emotion, movement, and expression. Further, the body occupies the central point in most contemporary art both through its presence or absence.

Anahita's analysis thus creates layers of philosophical discussion, from the intimate and the particular to the significant and the universal. What Anahita perceives, in my view, is a reflexive stance through her painting which could embrace a multitude of interpretations. While we are not able to see her painting, we are able to use the idea of the body, in her case the female body, to imagine and contemplate the ordinary and the epic, the sacred and the abused, and so on. Anahita is, in a way, opening the way for us to read into the dynamics of her psychosocial, interrelating the process of her inner and outer worlds, through a short reflexive and critical ethnographic text. We thus understand while she paints nude images of her own body intuitively and as an 'a priori' concept, it is possible that she brings into the argument a whole host of theoretical references including the relevance of the figure to the Classical canon in art history and all that it represents.

We also learn from the text that no matter how unacceptable the idea of the nude in the public arena in Iran, Anahita is autonomously engaging with the bigger world, depicting it through her creative act and in this instance her very brief account of her painting. This ethnographic text thus becomes symbolic of the ability to shift one's intellectual location, even if through articulating a strong idea, in this instance from the picture world of her painting we cannot see, to us through words. The desire to be autonomous, and to act autonomously is evident in her brief text. These are the qualities which are both pursued and practised widely by Iranian women in the contemporary period and Anahita brings them to the attention of the analytical reader.

I shall conclude this section with the following statement in order to consolidate the points I have made in the foregoing paragraphs. Here, we meet Pariush, a female art tutor and lecturer who also teaches at Al-Zahra University for Women. She provides the reader with a critical and reflexive address through engaging with her understanding of the abstract qualities of Islamic philosophy and thought, but also demonstrates gendered identity, Muslim identity, and politics at her locale. She reiterates that her mind will not be interfered with! Her text, however, is emblematic of so many million women in the Muslim world who practise Islam in ways meaningful to them, rather than blindly following instructions given by mediators.

I have been teaching art for the last 18 years at two universities; whilst also practising and regularly exhibiting painting, I am exploring ideas of scale and geometry at present. The famous saying from Madineh Fazeleh *'do not enter if you do not grasp geometry'* has a symbolic meaning for me and is never far from my mind…. As you know Madinah in Saudi Arabia is a holy shrine and mosque and the place where Prophet Mohammad was buried. It is a highly regarded venerated venue for those who attend the Hajj ceremonies in Mecca in Saudi Arabia. I take this statement about geometry as a sacred philosophy and work with it. At the moment my paintings are about intertwined geometrical forms in strong reds and blues; these gradually become more abstract. My paintings are large scale, often 3 to 4 metres long and 2 metres high.

As a tutor, I design the courses I teach according to my education, my understanding of art and art history, and my expertise. I insist on being autonomous in what I teach. I love being around my students, they give me energy, I get up in the morning and put my lipstick on and wear my headscarf and go to work, I need the income. I have supported my family financially all my married life and I am proud to have helped my students to go to Japan to do MA degrees, two of them have got scholarships to do PhDs there. Sadly, in the West, there is no consciousness of Iranian women like me, and our culture. There are considerable numbers of us contributing and defying restrictions as much as we can.... I for one refuse to apply self-censorship and insist on thinking freely, despite the head scarf. You cannot touch my mind.

The Derridean concepts of deconstruction and différance

Complementing the foregoing ethnographic approaches and their critical-analytical stance is the poststructuralist paradigm in contemporary critical theories and philosophy. Whilst poststructuralism does not wholly negate structuralism and its tradition-based and linear philosophical approach, it nevertheless problematizes the structuralists' absolutist convictions in logic, their often binary oppositions, their essentialist hermeneutic hierarchies, and their recognition of the universality of Western traditions in thought.

The Derridean concepts of deconstruction and différance have been the focus of my poststructuralist enquiries, particularly where he expands on the phenomenology movement founded by Edmund Husserl, and evolves and develops such ideas beyond the deconstruction of language and grammar. Derrida's approach is, in my view, an invitation to place focus on the science of phenomena as detailed description of conscious experience, without recourse to over-interpretation, metaphysical assumptions, and predicted traditional philosophical questions. With such a philosophical background, Jacques Derrida has put forward the concept of deconstruction or deconstructive reading, also referred to as the 'ethics of deconstruction', as a means of analysing human experience within the contexts of space and time (Cohen, 2001; Bullock and Trombley, 2000; Derrida, 1998; Derrida, 1997; Norris, 1987; Benjamin, 1997). This form or attitude towards the analysis of phenomena has proved particularly vital in studying Tehran because it resists 'Othering' in relation to ideological convictions, forms of worship, and exoticizing traditions outside the 'Western norms'.

In Derridian terms, deconstruction as a form of dividing literary texts into parts, or simply categorising them under lists and headings, is limiting the complexity of their meanings. We are recommended to pause, drop the hierarchic analysis of thought in the form of tradition in canonical discourses in literary texts, and take up the reading and re-reading of their margins looking for layers of meaning. Deconstruction in its Derridean sense is not a form of linear disassembling of parts, nor is it a system of backtracking and putting ideas sequentially or chronologically. Deconstructive reading emerges as an ethical demand. It aims at revealing what might appear insignificant to form complex and multiple perspectives. It takes into consideration the contradictions in social behaviours, noting gaps and uncertainties as well as certainties. It promotes vigilance in details of critical incidents, and reflects on personal and collective histories in order to construct layers in epistemologies.

Related to the deconstructive theories is the conception of 'la différance' as a contemporary and politically alert philosophical orientation. It was first put forward by Derrida in 1966 at Johns Hopkins University in a paper regarding literary texts and language. This was further developed in his teachings and writings in France and presented again in 1968 with wider political bearings, more inclusively applied to the arts, social sciences, law, etc., aiming to acknowledge the dimensions of world cultures and identities (Critchly, 1999). This form of inclusion, transcending the centrality of literary texts in academic discourses and searching and contemplating knowledge from diverse sources is particularly significant in inter-disciplinarity in research. La différance continues the deconstructive reading of texts whilst making references to 'trace', 'mark' and 'time'. It regards meaning in phenomena to be at once different or 'differential' and 'deferred'. Différance, as is perceived by Norris (1987), is a phonetic re-arrangement of the words 'differ' and 'defer' as a marker or reminder of how layers of experience, traces and residues of facts and time might affect meaning. In real terms, these suggest layered and unending histories, considering the spatio-temporal qualities in social behaviours, ideologies, and traditions. The notion of différance, therefore, alerts hermeneutics to the shift and 'movement' (Cohen, 2001) in meaning, allowing for a degree of open-endedness. This is how Derrida himself refers to it:

> Différance is a network of differentially signifying traces of meaning implying limitlessness of contexts; 'the effort to take this limitless context into account: la prise en compte de ce contexte sans bord'.

> (Critchly, 1999: 38; citing Derrida)

Whilst such contentions of limitlessness of contexts and perceptions carry the danger of over-relativism, it nevertheless alerts the researcher to the data's potential for multiple readings and dimensions. This was a point of discovery in the study where a cluster of detailed ethnographic texts were selected and juxtapositioned under the heading of 'Contradictory Spaces'. The experiences of two male tutors around the age of fifty and one female student about to graduate illuminated shifts in political ideologies and political design, as well as the shortfall in the curriculum, books, and visual teaching aids.

The three participants in this instance received their art training at Tehran University Visual Arts Department at different times. The male professor, who is also the director of the department, gave detailed accounts of his origins and piety, the holy city of Mashhad in the north-eastern province of Khorasan, and analysed the staffing and curriculum structures in relation to the new Islamic regime. He further addressed the impact of the post 1980 'cultural revolution' or 'enghelab-e farhangi' which was imposed on all educational institutions in Iran in order to cleanse them of unwanted secular elements. The professor further discussed his Islamist principles and their interrelationship with the conception of the 1979 Revolution, and how as a student in the department he had supported and fought for every aspect of that Revolution, and subsequently succeeded in securing a scholarship for a doctoral degree in Paris. Dedicated to the student body, and proud of his particular version of Islamic thought and practice, he considered his identity and his secure tenure prospects and position legitimately interconnected with the governmental ideologies, at least publicly. The other tutor, also a student in the department at the outset of the 1979 Revolution, gave a detailed account of his upbringing in a traditional family in a north-eastern province, the history of the political struggles and interventions of the student body at Tehran University at the time of the Revolution, and the conflicts between the Mojahed and Islamist groups at the time. He said that he was profoundly interested in art learning and training and did not belong to either group, seeking out only those scholars who were teaching him art. This second 'sessional tutor' (at another institution) saw the 'cultural revolution' as a process of *cleansing*, where anyone not dem-onstrating their allegiance to the new regime publicly, was, at the very least, pushed out of the system altogether. He pointed out that his identity was interconnected to his art and his 'colour pallet', and his private students who knew him as a practising and exhibiting artist rather than a governmental and religious zealot. The perspectives within these views enrich the meaning and the consequences of the 1979 Revolution at Tehran University. They further indicate the current conflict of identities experienced in the renamed Faculty of Visual Arts.

The third person in this cluster of ethnographic texts was a young female sculpture student who gave detailed accounts of what it was like to be a student at Tehran University currently. She spoke at length about how university education has given her the understanding and self-knowledge to have a voice, and how she expresses her ideas through art and registers her opinions regarding society. Whilst not using the word identity, the sculpture student analysed her experience in the processes of acquiring a meaningful identity through voice, registering ideas and opinions. Like many of the students observed, she appeared to have been taught well, and learnt well. She spoke of the excessive weight given to the study of theory in the curriculum, and how she could not understand why the history of the Islamic Revolution was included in such theoretical teachings year after year. Like all her peers she had studied the latter in detail repeatedly at secondary school too. Further, the presence of the ethical or moral guardians, the 'heraasat', as minders of dress codes and social behaviours between the sexes were amongst her concerns. Above all, however, the shortages in books and visual materials were a big worry. The latter are censored if containing nudity, and are consequently subjected to censorship and what is considered and labelled as 'not suitable' or 'problematic'. From a traditional and low income background, she spoke about how she has had to persuade her father to accept university art education as valid. This is how she related her work:

My four year period studying art at university has persuaded my father that yes, I have chosen a life direction for myself and that it's alright.... Especially since the day I won a prize for my installation with needles. I created a very narrow path with white polystyrene walls, at the end of which were scattered one thousand soft new green leaves...but the walls were pierced with over one thousand large quilting needles which I had asked my father who is a tailor to buy for me. I am also preparing for an installation of seven white steps covered in needles that lead you to a white wall which does not go anywhere!

At the moment I am following a few strands for my finals: land art, environmental art, the ephemeral, 'site' specificity, and performance art. I am designing a vertical sculpture in adobe mud bricks whose centre would be in ice; as the process of melting takes place this sculpture will start to disintegrate, slowly collapsing on itself. The adobe bricks will be made of the earth I would have dug up at the site of the sculpture...so the base of the vertical is in the hollow, and subterranean...viewed from a distance the section of the sculpture that is in the 'dug up recess', the roots as it were, would not be seen, the sculpture would be just a presence on the horizon for a limited time. I am making arrangements for this to be documented by video. Calculations of scale, time, weather conditions and temperatures are important parts of the processes. I am interested and moved by Andy Goldsworthy's ice sculptures and am translating an article by Anthony Gormley regarding his views on the 'site' of a sculpture. This takes a long time as my English is not that good, it is what I learnt at school and university.

Thus, the conceptual tools, whether reflexive and critical ethnographies, or deconstruction and 'la différance', urge one to be inclusive, to seek particularities of experience, to note sources of individual identities, to view time and space as significant, and observe the notion of art teaching and learning multi-dimensionally. They have provided for the ability to defer the accepted norms of right and wrong in meaning-making, hoping for ideologies to reveal and unmask themselves without over-interpretation. Such orientations might also present significant ethical value, safeguarding the integrity and wholesomeness of each ethnographic text, recognizing their autonomy, and resisting both Othering and exoticizing.

These conceptual tools alert the researcher to understand the complexities present in the field. I believe this notion of understanding could be compared to deconstructing a painting. In a painting, reading starts with recognizing the space of the canvas and reading form and structure within it. In a painting, the physical potential and textural qualities in paint, values in colour, their saturation and luminosity, and the emotional power associated with them might be established according to their positioning. In such analogy deconstruction transforms colours into ideas, shades of dark for example, dealing with the sensual qualities they might project, the qualities they might induce in their neighbours, as well as a hermeneutic memory system for the whole painting which would be inclusive of their frequency or rhythm occurrences of paints as well as forms. Such judgements may never be final however, since the psychological, art historical notions, as well as the contexts of the painter and the viewer, the context of the site of the exhibition, and the quality of light might promote further readings. The reading of a good painting continues beyond the time of viewing and the limitations of the canvas.

The development of the concepts of 'text'

In the previous section, I have presented and discussed 'ethnographic texts' represented in words and not in their given form verbally. I would wish to suggest that texts are means of communicating and interpreting ideas and knowledge and that they might also be given in visual forms as in photo essays or art videos, etc. Indeed texts could be performed, and interpreted as in a declamation, or they could relate movement in space as in 'performance' art which is increasingly being used to convey and interpret meaning. As Geertz contends, social acts of being in the world are 'text-analogous' (Geertz, 2000: 17). Derrida too considers human activity, whether political, economic, historical, or socio-institutional to possess meaning and subject of interpretation (Derrida, 1999).

As a researcher and practising artist, my work embodies such ideas. These ideas form my mindscape and I do not discard any part of this mindscape whether working in the studio, or gathering and developing data at the site of social-scientific enquiry. Indeed I regard the processes of the creative act as social-scientific engagement. I also recognize the power of intention, and the fact that once ideas, as forms of knowledge, are delivered to others with intention, they possess meaning and have the ability to convey that meaning to varying degrees. Such notions can easily be examined through the volumes and libraries of critical and speculative material written on art and its power and meaning, both in its primitive and modern forms. An art object thus possesses textual and inter-textual qualities because when one works on objects or ideas one is constantly referring to the histories of art and the individual. Serious art, by which I mean sustained and focused work, is intended to communicate a message, albeit not in the written form. I further believe that once an idea is perceived, considered, ordered, thought through, adopted, and executed and projected it will possess meaning and might be 'read' as text. Such a stance has been significant in the production of a multi-media multi-text thesis where interviews and statement, oral histories, photo essays, moving image, and art objects have been assembled and counted as data in the processes of enquiry. They have all been contemplated to extract meaning.

My clay sculptures, 33 fragments of female form hung in a large cluster (5 x 5 metres) from the ceiling in the centre of a large gallery in Tehran, were the outward expressions of my mindscape, especially during the processes of interviews in Tehran. They referenced the female body, the relevance and aspects of which have been briefly discussed above in relation to Anahita's statement and painting. Not only did the sculptures become a means for accessing self-definition and self-knowledge through sustained practice in the studio over a period of one year, but they also led me to try to imagine and understand the strengths and vulnerabilities of the female participants in Tehran, resisting restrictions both artistically and socio-politically. I became more alert to their rigour and strife for expression, despite limitations. And above all I better understood the vital role art practice can have in determining and articulating aspects of one's experience and complex identities.

The sculptures further indicated a shared cultural heritage and geography bringing the researched and researcher together in a shared space. This is because in a highly abstract way, I further interconnect the installation of 33 fragments of female form, suspended in space in rhythm and time, to a symbolic state of being referencing collective sensibilities and alertness towards Persian classical and modern literary heritage. The female essence, both in its physical and metaphysical forms, is a concept often referred to in Iranian poetry engaging with bodies of ideas such as the 'dance of the beloved', 'ascendance' and 'light'. Such notions and cultural nuances are deeply rooted in one's upbringing and collective psyche and were rigorously contemplated during the making of the works in my studio in Canterbury. As the sculptures developed, I would increasingly recall such vital elements in my my personal experience and history. I would then register and inscribe them visually and materially, in clay in the space of the studio. Similarly, the qualities of colour in stones and architectural remains in archaic sites of Persian antiquity prompted me to recreate something in clay which might, in some way, be connected to those origins. My sculptures were thus intentionally presented as a meeting place of ideas, bearing formal references to art-historical precedence, as well as suggesting visual metaphors and visual inscriptions in clay to the participants in Tehran. Whilst they were from a sensory non-verbal world of perceptions where their execution rotated on a triple axis of the experiences and histories of the researcher, the history of art, and the experiences and histories of the participants in Tehran, they reflected our continued dialogue based on sensibilities from a particular locale.

The sculptural work thus became a bold visual statement about female form and its collective emblematic meanings. I created a common ground, and the work was received as a text message to a dear friend. Above all, in Tehran, the work was understood by artists and the public alike, and in passing I heard a comment by a female writer with a critical eye: 'This body of work belongs here, it should not leave this land'. It was clear that the sculptures had been read by many as a familiar document registering experience, shared experience, inscribing one's origins of identity, and conveying a sense of belonging through art.

Conclusion

In this chapter I hope to have shown how multi-perspective and multi-source theories and methodologies can enrich the processes and impact of the message of research. Such methodological scaffolding has primarily rotated on the triple axis of critical and reflexive ethnographies, the poststructuralist Derridean concepts of deconstruction and différance, and the idea of 'text'. These have allowed for the illumination of identities, the location of the participants including the researching-artist, and a dialogue and reciprocity between them. Furthermore, the site and elements in the study have assumed fluid qualities inclusive of Tehran and Canterbury, and outcomes in visual, sculptural, and literary texts. Thus, contemporary research gains strength through juxtapositioning of ideas rather than limitations and 'Othering'.

From Tehran, I hope I have shown the complexity, diversity, and multi-dimensional aspects of the perceptions of art students and their tutors under Islam. Though few in numbers, the experiences related in the data illuminate areas of contested identities, reason for political debate, as well as discussions vital to broader discourses in art. The statements and views presented go beyond geographical boundaries and engage with geopolitics, the canon of art practice and art history, and the notion of autonomy. The participants in Tehran have demonstrated how identities are related to experience; this is disclosed in the accounts and experiences related by the two male and one female tutors, as well as Maryam's statement.

The data further suggests that cultural nuances are indicative of origins of experience and identity, and that the ethnographic self-observation in the studio might end in sculptural texts and become instrumental to register the researcher's presence and the ways in which she makes meaning.

I hope I have demonstrated how ethnographic texts cannot be viewed simply in isolation and how time and place and the condition of a particular locale are ultimately connected to the bigger picture, the human story, experience and condition.

Note

1. Jihad is an Arabic word which simply means striving for betterment. Jahad is the Farsi pronunciation of the same word. The 'educational jahad' or 'jahad-e danesh-gahi' is a governmental organization that provides opportunities, and some financial assistance too if necessary, to vetted applicants. It creates an advisory/consultancy/tutorial space in almost any discipline. It has been particularly beneficial to re-habilitate many soldiers from the Iran-Iraq war to come into terms with their traumas and disabilities through education. This facility is also highly appreciated by

many who have faced hardships through lack of opportunities; it has been part of the message of the Revolution to create such opportunities for the 'disadvantaged'. It is, however, generally understood that Jahad beneficiaries, at least outwardly and visibly, demonstrate their support for the government and its policies or stance on interpreting moral/ethical codes of behaviour. Participating in pro-government demonstrations, attending mass prayers and adhering to dress codes for women, in particular, are also implied.

References

Benjamin, A., 'Eisenman and the Housing of Tradition', in Leach, N. (ed.), *Rethinking Architecture* (London: Routledge, 1997), 283–379.

Bullock, A., and Trombley, S. (eds.), *New Fontana Dictionary of Modern Thought* (London: Harper Collins, 2000).

Carspecken, P.F., *Critical Ethnography in Educational Research: A Theoretical and Practical Guide* (New York: Routledge Chaplin, 1996; Harper, 2000).

Cohen, T., *Jacques Derrida and the Humanities: A Critical Reader* (Cambridge: Cambridge University Press, 2001).

Critchly, S., *The Ethics of Deconstruction* (Edinburgh: Edinburgh University Press, 1999).

Derrida, J., 'Point de folie—Maintenant l'architecture', in N. Leach (ed.), *Rethinking Architecture: A Reader in Cultural Theory* (London: Routledge, 1997b), 324–347.

Derrida, J., *Monolingualism of the Other or the Prosthesis of Origin* (California: Stanford University Press, 1998).

Geertz, C., *Available Light Anthropological Reflections on Philosophical Topics* (Princeton: Princeton University Press Harper, 2001).

Jenks, C., 'The Centrality of the Eye in Western Culture', in C. Jenks (ed.), *Visual Culture* (London: Routledge, 1995), 1–12.

Kincheloe, J.L., and McLaren, P., 'Rethinking Critical Theory and Qualitative Research', in K. Denzin and S. Lincoln (eds.), *Handbook of Qualitative Research*, 2e (London: Sage Publications Inc, 2000), 279–313.

Ladson-Billings, G., 'Racialized Discourses and Ethnic Epistemologies', in K. Denzin and S. Lincoln (eds.), *Handbook of Qualitative Research*, 2e (London: Sage Publications, 2000), 257–277.

Lincoln, Y.S., and Guba, E.G., 'Paradigmatic Controversies, Contradictions, and Emerging Confluences', in K. Denzin and S. Lincoln (eds.), *Handbook of Qualitative Research*. 2e (London: Sage Publications Inc, 2000), 163–188.

Norris, N., *Derrida* (Cambridge Massachusetts: Harvard University Press, 1987).

Pink, S., *Doing Visual Ethnography* (London: Sage, 2004).

Rose, G., *Visual Methodologies* (London: Sage, 2004).

Tedlock, B., 'Ethnography and Ethnographic Representation', in K. Denzin and S. Lincoln (eds.), *Handbook of Qualitative Research* 2e (London: Sage Publications, 2000), 455–486.

8

Performing methodological activities in post-colonial ethnographic encounters

Examples from Oaxaca, Mexico

ÁNGELES CLEMENTE AND MICHAEL J. HIGGINS

Introduction

Our contribution to this volume on the perils, pitfalls and reflexivity of qualitative research in education is to explain how we have dealt with these issues in our ethnographic encounters dealing with language and literacy activities in the post-colonial multilingual and multicultural context of Oaxaca, Mexico.

The city of Oaxaca is a metropolitan area with a current population of over half a million residents. It is the capital of the state Oaxaca, which is located in the southwestern region of Mexico and has a population of over 3.2 million people. It is well-known for its ethnic diversity, colonial architecture, ecological variety and extreme poverty. The city of Oaxaca is the political, commercial and communication center of the state. In addition, it has many of the problems associated with urbanization in Mexico: shortage of housing, and limited employment possibilities for 'popular' classes, traffic congestion, and political protests (Hernandez Diaz, 2007). Pollution and water shortages are increasingly problematic, as well.

This is the context in which we have carried out various methodological performances dealing with the following ethnographic encounters: an overall investigation into the composition and performance in English of the students at the language center at the state university in Oaxaca (Clemente and Higgins, 2008); an emerging encounter on cultural literacy practices among inmates at the state prison in Oaxaca (Clemente and Higgins, 2009); and an account of poor young urban students learning English in a local primary school in the city of Oaxaca (Clemente, Dantas, and Higgins, in press).

These three ethnographic studies have provided the information for the five illustrations of methodological performance that we will be analyzing in this chapter. Before these examples, we will provide a short conceptual argument to explain what we mean by ethnographic encounters (Fabian, 2007), and how, because methods are part of this process, they become performative activities. In the conclusion to this chapter, we will show how these assumptions are connected to the epistemological and political focus of this volume.

Fabian stresses that 'ethnography is a product of interaction, with speaking as its major, though not the only, medium; it is dialogical. What we take away from research as data is only sometimes found, most often it is made' (2007: 13). Thus, this 'emphasis on communication and language in action' made social scientists 'realize how much of cultural knowledge and hence ethnography is performative' and 'what we learn [as social scientists] often does not come as responses to our questions but is enacted in, and mediated by, events which we may trigger but cannot really control' (ibid). What we refer to as our methods—interviews, observations, and protocols—are *ethnographic performances*. Such a position accepts and recognizes that ethnographic means of representations are partial and contingent; that is, the representations are constrained by the time and space realities of both the ethnographer and those of the ethnography and are contingent upon the actual social and material realities of all those involved in producing the narrative. Further, although traditional forms of data collection and composition can be critically used (interviews, observations, participation and residency within the ethnographic context), there is also a seeking for *ethnographic praxis*. Methodologically, this involves opening the interviewing process to reflective dialogue between all the participants in the endeavour, sharing and collaborating on how the range and style of ethnography can be developed, and collectively searching for forms of multimodal expressions of all the actors' activities. This further assumes that the ethnographic shape of these various activities will and can be of use to the social actors in developing their own critical reflections on their everyday lives. In turn, they can use such reflections as forms of empowerment towards their own expression of praxis.

Fabian states that the 'goal of anthropology or [its] challenge is to understand (and demonstrate) humanity's unity;...to attain this goal depends on recognizing the presence or co-temporaneity of the peoples whom we study' (2007: 3). To paraphrase Fabian's argument, we could say that the qualitative research studies in education have their empirical foundation in ethnographic research that is carried out as communicative interaction which requires the ethnographers to recognize the people whom they study as their coevals. It is within these ethnographic performative dynamics that the co-equivalency of all the participants is composed. That is, there is neither an analytical nor a material separation of time and space between those involved in these encounters, but rather collaborative movements through shared time and space that allow for an 'empirical' representation of these performances (Clemente and Higgins, 2009).

Given these assumptions, methods are not external procedures that frame the research, but part of the collaborative performance of the ethnographic encounter. Kumaravadivelu in several works (2003 and 2006) has developed a discourse that he refers to as post-methodology, in which he suggests that the context of both the researcher and the researched should set, and encourage, appropriate strategies of investigation. That context would include the social, cultural and political realities of those involved in the research. Furthermore, he stresses that there are no sets of techniques or stratagems to follow, but that one has to make various critical and reflective choices as to how to attain the appropriate information and data that can best represent the social dynamics one has been investigating (Kumaravadivelu, 2007). That is, one needs to be able to perform methods that are socially and ethnically contextualized to co-equivalent realities of all the participants within the ethnographic encounter.

Therefore, what we are about to present is a series of ethnographic activities about the encounters mentioned above. We will not be presenting methodological recipes, nor a set of 'how to' rules for data collection. We will show how within these activities, various methodological opportunities emerged through the performative interactive dynamics of all the participants. It is our ethnographic style to use the information (data) that emerges in these interactions to build or compose narratives that attempt to represent these overall encounters (Clemente and Higgins, 2009). For heuristic purposes, we present the following five illustrations of how we 'collected' our data.

1. Interactive data collection: Summer school in the state prison

We will illustrate what we mean by interactive data collection from an ethnographic encounter involving summer school for the inmates' children at the state prison. As will be discussed at length below, we also worked with the inmates themselves.

The social work department at the state prison asked us to provide four English teachers (for four different levels: pre-elementary, Year 1–2, Year 3–4, Year 5–6) for the summer school that is implemented every year at the state prison. These courses have been one of the solutions for the overcrowded conditions of the prison each summer when the inmates' families come from different parts of the state to visit them. Since summer allows the families (spouses and children) of the inmates more time to visit, and given their limited financial means (if they are not from the city, they cannot afford to go back and forth to their hometowns, nor can they pay for hotels in the city), they are allowed to stay in the prison. This year, more than a hundred children, ranging in ages from two to fifteen years old, enrolled in the prison summer school. The program runs for

eight weeks during the months of July and August. We posted
an invitation at the *Facultad de Idiomas* asking for four student-
teachers in their last year of their TESOL program who wanted
to carry out the social service requirement as English teachers in
the state prison. Eight very eager students applied. We decided
to team teach the courses assigning two of them to each level.

We did not know the social, cultural and economic background
of the children, but we supposed that they were from fragile
social situations; thus, we thought that the way to teach these
children had to be different. First, because the children had to
deal with a parent who had not been a daily presence in their
everyday lives; and secondly, since they were now visiting that
person in prison, they had to learn how to deal with that context
as part of their new everyday routines. We felt that these English
classes should not be an imposition of language and content but
a way to offer them another communicative tool (additional to
their first and/or second language) to express themselves.

Thus, we made decisions about teaching methodology and
class content. In terms of teaching methodology, we asked the
students-teachers to carry out their different teaching/learning
activities with a bilingual approach. In this case we define a
bilingual approach as the use of code-mixing Spanish, the *lingua
franca* of both the teachers and students, with English, the
language to be learnt. We thought that by using both languages,
the students would learn the new language more easily and
would be more confident in using it. We hoped that since the
class was not to be monolingual, they would feel free to be more
creative in their languages (Canagarajah, 2006; Sommer, 2004).
This resulted in very lively classes, in which the students who
had an indigenous language as their L1, felt free to use it and
even to teach the other students some words.

In terms of teaching content, we thought that Freire's
participatory approach could be adapted for a content-based
English curriculum to establish the conditions for making the
English content meaningful to these students (Freire and
Macedo, 1987). One of the main assets of Freire's approach is

that the content is not predetermined by the teacher but defined by the students according to the issues that interest them (Larsen-Freeman, 2000). Thus, we decided that the first session would deal with the students' concept of English, and what and why they wanted (or did not want) to learn English. The following sessions were dedicated to their identity (who they are, where they were born, etc.), context (hometown, house, community), household (who they live with, what are their relationships), everyday activities (at home and at school), leisure activities (during school breaks, at home and in the neighbourhood) and their future (what they want to be, where they want to live and with whom).

In order for these topics to be worked on in a participatory mode, the student-teachers planned activities that allowed the students to participate with their own information and knowledge. For example, when teaching the vocabulary related to *the house*, within the topic of context, instead of providing an illustration of a house with all the different lexical items to be taught, the students-teachers planned an activity where the students were to provide the drawings of their houses with the different items that were in their own homes. That way, the children were in charge of defining what vocabulary they were to learn in the English class. Another good example was the teaching of *the family*, in which we consciously avoided the presentation of a 'typical family' (nuclear family, heterosexual couples as parental unit, two or three kids, everybody looking happy). Instead, students were asked who they lived with, and from there activities, such as, choosing from magazine cuttings, drawing pictures or writing short paragraphs, were set up to describe their own individual families.

This encounter illustrates the performative quality of data collection through the coevalness of all the participants (Fabian, 2007). We and the student teachers explored how to provide adequate English classes for these young students that could also be a means to collect ethnographic data connected to the everyday lives of inmates' families, through the perceptions of their children. This required then that children were to have an equivalent role to play in how the classes were to be structured and what kinds of information was to be used. Further, the students and their families were aware that we also wanted to share this information through the development of a general ethnography on cultural literacy practices in the prison. Needless to say, the data was quite 'thick' due to the richness and complexity of the household funds of knowledge that the children drew upon, no matter how young they were or how humble their backgrounds were (Moll, Amanti, Neff, and Gonzales, 1992; Velez-Ibanez and Greenberg, 1992). We did not bring a set of methods to the class, but methods emerged in the interaction of all the participants sharing the same time and space. Further, this was an expression of how ethnographic praxis can develop. Through the interactive dynamics of all the participants, these classes were grounded in the needs of the students themselves and the future narratives to emerge from this project would be supported by the views and hopes of these children.

2. Composition of data:
Ethnographic portraits of language students

Our second example has as its objective to illustrate that in the composition of data even the most traditional researcher's roles are also performative. In doing our ethnography of the language centre, we carried out numerous lengthy interviews with several students from the first to the fifth years in the program. We already knew some of the students who were selected (some had been our research assistants) and others were referred to us either by other professors or some other students of the Centre. Because of publication space constraints, we chose six students for developing their ethnographic portraits and included them in the book we wrote on this project (see Clemente and Higgins, 2008). Choosing who was to be included and who was not, is a good example of the many ways in which the qualitative researchers impact the results of their investigations. In the case of this study, and we think that it is the same in many such studies, the decision was very difficult because every social actor has stories that deserve to be told. Moreover, we tried to avoid generalizations, for we did not want our selection to be regarded as 'a representative sample' of the Language Center students. Our goal was to depict the diversity of the student population of the institution. Based on that premise, we chose students from recognizable genders, from different social backgrounds (urban and rural), from different ethnicities (Chinantec, Triqui, Zapotec, Arabic-Spanish and Mestizo), from different social classes and from different sexual orientations.

We gathered, from the students, a variety of documents that were a mixture of writings that they had produced as part of their academic lives (assignments, class work, theses, etc.) or in response to a request from us (autobiographies, diaries, reflections on specific topics, etc.). After they had agreed to be part of the study, we asked them to write an autobiography, which served as the starting point for long conversations that took place over several months. It was interesting that, although the autobiographies were very useful to get to know the general background of the students, they often omitted basic data about themselves, such as ethnicity or social class. There were cases where some students did not mention their jobs or, even more ironically, one student failed to mention that she had a two year old child. We constantly stressed to these students that every part of their lives was relevant. At the beginning of the study, this caused some suspicion amongst them; they did not understand how aspects such as their ethnicity or their sexual orientation could be connected to their academic lives in the university.

When we considered that we had a thorough compound of data on them, we started the composition of their ethnographic portraits, which was basically a text written by us based on transcriptions of interviews dealing with their autobiographies, their written academic documents, their views on aspects of their everyday lives (in Oaxaca, in the university and in the Language

Centre) and how they perceived their present and future lives (as students, speakers and future teachers of English). Although the ethnographic portraits were full of direct quotations from the original documents, we were the ones who decided how to order the information, selected what to include and what to leave out, and added comments which reflected our perceptions of the content. However, at this stage, it was necessary to maintain constant communication with the students to be able to fill in gaps, ask for clarifications and check details. Once the portraits were finished, the students read them, agreed on the content, and made suggestions for editing or altering the text. In fact the students even suggested which pseudonyms they wanted to use.

Though these methodological activities were mostly traditional forms of ethnographic inquiry, they too were performative. The selection, development and composition of the portraits were a constant source of dynamic interaction between all of us. The student participants were aware that they were involved in a collaborative project with us and that the material developed was to be used in a book based on our ethnographic research. In fact, they used their editorial rights to alter or emphasize different aspects of their portraits. We also stressed that any questions that we asked of them, they were free to ask the same to us. Thus the interviews were more about the sharing of ideas, feelings and emotions than following rigid formats of questions and answers. It was in this context that, again, the coevalness was constructed between us and the students. This too was an expression of ethnographic praxis, in that these students were able to shape how they were to be represented in their respective portraits.

3. Context-driven dynamics: Unimagined everyday realities in the state prison

The third example is an illustration of what we refer to as the context driven dynamics of data collection. This involves trying to move beyond what the researchers imagine things to be, and allowing themselves to be more open to alternatives that they had not imagined. As mentioned earlier, we are currently carrying out a study in the state prison on Oaxaca. One goal of this study is to do research on the cultural practices of literacy (Purcell-Gates, 2007; Street 1995) of the inmates of this re-adaptation centre, as the prison is formally called. This type of study has been carried out in minority and marginal communities in different parts of the world (Purcell-Gates, 2007). However, it has not been carried out in a closed community such as a prison. We thought that the intrinsic features of this type of social group would reveal interesting aspects of literacy as a cultural practice. Our first presupposition was that, given the obvious confinement of the inmates, they would use their reading and writing abilities for communication and entertainment. However, soon we realized that this was not the case. To use Holliday's words (Chapter 1 in this volume), our initial vision, that incarcerated people write and read letters to communicate to the outside world, that they have limited resources for entertainment and that they have a lot of free time to read, had to be replaced with the reality that was emerging in our interaction with the inmates. That is, we had to submit to the performative realities of everyday life in the prison. The inmates told us that they did not write many letters, nor did they receive them. When we asked about the ways they communicate with the outside world, they said that they mainly used the phone. They have access to two direct lines that are connected to the interior of the prison and some of inmates are allowed to use cell phones. Most felt that it was a more effective means of communication and some admitted that they, and their relatives, were not very skilful in the genre of writing. Actually, one of them, trying to convince us of the fact that a phone call was more effective than a letter, told us about another inmate who regularly calls his mother, who lives in Oaxaca, to tell her that he is still in the States working hard. They also told us that whenever they needed to communicate with somebody they could not call, they sent verbal messages with their visiting relatives.

In relation to entertainment, we discovered that, first of all, they do not have a lot of free time. Most of them have to work as much as they can in order to provide some funds for their families (usually they were their providers before they were incarcerated) or for their basic needs in prison (soap and detergent, toilet paper, phone cards). One of the main ways to earn money is sewing footballs by hand. If one sews three balls a day, he can make 27 pesos (more or less two US dollars) a day. Most workers, in fact, can do three footballs a day. Although it is one of the hardest jobs there is to do there, most of them choose it because they do not need to invest any money. Outside vendors, who provide all the material, bring it into the prison and recruit those that want to work. When inmates find some time to relax, many organize a football or a basketball game. The ones that are too tired for running and jumping get together with someone that has permission to have a TV or a radio; others simply gather in pairs or small groups to chat.

By taking clues from the everyday life of inmates we encountered two very different cultural literacy practices. The first refers to how they deal with their particular legal situations. From the very moment they are arrested, each one of them is involved in a long chain of legal texts, either receiving them or writing them. This literacy chain is very particular in the sense that, even though they are the main addresser and addressee of this interaction, they hardly understand its content. As in many legal systems in other countries, in Mexico, third parties are supposed to make the communication flow. Mainly, these are either private lawyers or the court-appointed counsellors that act as mediators. One of their main functions is to explain the content of documents addressed to the inmates and write the ones that they may need. However, most of the inmates told us that they try to avoid lawyers as mediators because they are not trustworthy. They are well known for working for the person who makes the best offer (who in most cases is not the accused) or simply for taking the money of their incarcerated client without doing any work.

Thus, the inmates are left by themselves to work out their legal issues. In some cases, the inmates that consider themselves capable try to learn this legal discourse. In fact, we were told that the legal section in the prison's library is the one most consulted. However, in most of the cases the inmates ignore their legal situation, and with that, any documents that come with it.

The other example of literacy was completely unexpected. On one occasion, we were carrying out an interview with one of the inmates about his work sewing footballs. What we were trying to find out was what kinds of literacy were related to his work. We asked about reading or writing texts such as job contracts, pay stubs, receipts of materials and finished footballs, instruction manuals, lists of materials, etc. The answers were always negative. This job seems to be administered in a rather casual way and almost nothing is written. However, when we thought that the interview was finished, Rafa, the inmate doing the sewing, added: 'But I write things inside the balls. I am not sure if that counts'. More specifically, he shared that he writes, somewhat randomly, something inside a football. Then he closes it and puts it with the others that are ready to be delivered. He told us that he is careful and respectful with what he writes, which are phrases he has seen or thoughts that he likes to write down. He added that he had no public in mind nor did he think he was sending out 'messages in a bottle'. It just made him feel good.

Through these various forms of informal interaction with these inmates we have become aware of the unexpected realities of their everyday lives. Instead of trying to find what we had imagined, we had to let ourselves be open to the unimagined within this social context (Clemente and Higgins, 2009). We imagined that inmates would have significant amounts of free time, when it was quite the opposite. We knew that the inmates had to deal with the reality of being physically confined within the structures of the prison, but we had not imagined that they would also be incarcerated within the textual domains of the legal discourse. Nor had we imagined the imaginative ways inmates could move beyond the walls of prison, such as Rafa's messages inside the footballs. These activities are strong examples of Fabian's claim that what we derive from our ethnographic encounters does not come from strict adherence to methodological recipes but emerges from the performative interaction of the participants.

4. Forms of Emergence of Local Knowledge: The Monsters in the Primary School

Part of what we mean by coevalness, is the openness of the researchers to doubt their own interpretation and contrast it with the views of the other social actors participating in the study. The following example illustrates this point.

In a study carried out in a local primary school, Yedani, one Facultad de Idiomas student-teacher, was teaching English to a fifth year class, in which most of the students were male and came from *la Ciudad de los Ninos*, a shelter for homeless and abandoned boys. Knowing that her students enjoyed drawing more than writing, Yedani asked them to draw a monster, in order to practice the vocabulary for parts of the body. Their drawings were very interesting and varied (Clemente, Dantas and Higgins, 2009). The students in using their local knowledge were able to complete their assignments in very creative ways: they referred to their collectible cards; showed their favourite characters from cartoons, movies or videogames; used tattoo/graffiti graphics; or offered what for them were punk looks that included details of body piercing. Among these details, there was one that caught our attention: the high frequency of scars in most of the drawings (See Fig. 1).

Figure 1. Example of monster with scars

For us, this had a direct connection with Frankenstein, the 'famous' character created by Mary Shelly. However, when we talked to the children about their monsters, it was clear that they had not seen or heard about Frankenstein. What they told us was that, due to the personalities and behaviour of their monsters (troublemakers, fighters, night-prowlers, and cannibals), the scars were the result of their frequent streets fights. Thus the scars, we found, had no link to the chirurgical interventions of Shelly's character.

This mismatch between perceptions about monsters cannot be explained as a lack of world knowledge on the part of the children, but as a good example of how, first of all, the previous knowledge of the researcher can interfere in the appropriate interpretation of the information, and secondly, how valuable it is to go back to the participants to obtain the necessary information to make sense of the data. That is, since both, we as the ethnographers and they as students, were co-participants in the encounter, the analysis emerged from our performative interactions, and not from the authority of our singular perceptions (Fabian, 2007).

5. Coevalness in Data Collection: A Creative Writing Course in the State Prison

The last example describes the way we—primarily Angeles Clemente—carried out a creative writing course in the State Prison. Requested by some inmates interested in writing, Angeles organized a course for them to write poetry and narratives. The course was begun in March 2009 and it was to end by September 2009 (when they could share their work with the prison community during the festivities of the prison). However, the participants have asked to continue the course after September. Their goal is to get enough material to publish a book, provided that they can find somebody to sponsor it.

Thirteen people showed up for the first session, but half of them did not continue. The reasons were different: some of them could not find the time to write; others thought that it was too difficult; and some decided they did not want to be with inmates they did not like. There were a total of seven inmates who stayed: five from those who showed up from the first class and another two who heard about the course and joined later. The group is very diverse: there are five men and two women; two of the students have university degrees, three have finished high school, and two have attended secondary school. Two of them have been in prison for more than seven years, while the others are relatively recent arrivals. Also, we learnt that three of the students had had some previous experiences in writing, while for the other five, this was the first time they had tried creative writing.

The way Angeles worked it out was rather simple. Following the example of a colleague's creative writing class (Clemente and Higgins, 2008), she taught them how to develop word clusters. She chose a word (such as *eating, pain, table*), and the students made their own personal connections with these terms. Their individual clusters were very different from each other. Their homework was to write a poem using most of the words of the cluster. Angeles would collect their poems and take them home to work with. At the beginning, some of them did not feel very comfortable working in verses and stanzas, so they wrote little paragraphs, while others, following traditional concepts of poetry, tried to construct rhymed verses which resulted in very complicated pieces.

One aspect that Angeles found difficult was correcting their writings. She was aware that they were expecting not only words of encouragement but also her concrete feedback. However, she did not feel like writing on their poems—changing, moving, adding or crossing out words—the way she would do with her language classes at the university. Fortunately, she came up with an alternative way to present her views about their creations: she took their poems home, read them, transcribed them on to the computer, and made the changes she considered necessary while always being careful not to change their content. When she felt happy with the outcome, she scanned the original poem and placed it on the same page as her 'corrected' version so that they could all see the two poems side by side (see Appendix). In the following class they would compare the two versions, highlighting the differences. Angeles always made sure to ask the students if they agreed with each one of the changes. She stressed that they were free to stay with their original version. At the beginning, they tended to accept almost all her changes, but soon they began to show more assertiveness, some students telling her, in a polite way, that they liked both the versions, while others saying overtly that they preferred their version over hers.

Though all the examples in this chapter illustrate what we have been referring to as the coevalness of ethnographic encounters, the creative writing course illustrates how through such intimate interactions, different forms of data can emerge. Angeles's account of how she structured the class, worked with the students, composed suggestive alternatives to their poems, and how they accepted or altered those suggestions, is a concrete example of how all the participants of this encounter were sharing the same time and space. More important, in the discussion about the clusters, the presentation of poems, and the interactive dialogues on the final versions, a wealth of personal information was exchanged, everyone sharing feelings about emotions, hopes, fears, and what the future could be. Often, the inmates would say that they needed to write a book so those on the outside could know who they were and what they had to deal with in their everyday lives in the prison. In this context of sharing the same time and space all the participants came to know themselves and each other in different and new ways. In the coevalness of these encounters, we as the ethnographers were not distance observers but collaborators with these inmates in constructing a stage where all of us could perform in a more humane style that could be associated with life behind prisons walls.

Conclusion

In this chapter, we have tried to illustrate the dynamics of coevalness in a range of ethnographic encounters in varied settings in Oaxaca, Mexico. We shared the same material and analytical time with those working in these encounters, as different ways of collecting data emerged. That is our methodology. It is not a set of rules or frameworks, but a diversity of performative activities that allows for data to emerge during the interactive dynamics. Due to contextual elements, the final performances involved various further writing and interpreting activities where these encounters were formed into ethnographic narratives.

The question we would like to pose as a means of conclusion to this chapter is: what are the times and spaces we share with the diversity of authors and their works in this volume? We think that the times and spaces we share derive from the reality that we are all living in a postcolonial world anchored by a globalized political economy (Castells, 2000). This is a world in which our everyday lives transpire in a multilingual/multicultural context, that is, the social fields that compose these globalized postcolonial spaces are filled with a diversity of cultural worlds that are mediated by the social dynamics of difference, inequality and disconnection (García Canclini, 2004). It has also been suggested that there is a world of interculturalism, a quest for forms of equivalent differences and substantive connections (Dietz, 2003). Within these existing forms of cultural diversity (gender, sexuality, ethnicity, social class and ableness) numerous practices are being composed, encouraging various forms of negotiation that seek to go beyond existing forms of power and authority. It is within these various social folds where the interplays between language, agency, identity and culture are performed.

One of the hegemonic struggles taking place within these spaces is what Mignolo refers to as the colonial difference. *Colonial difference* refers to the geopolitics of the production of knowledge and the question of who has the power to claim the authority of knowledge. It is those in the metropolitan zones who assert this right to produce universal knowledge that dominates the local knowledges of those in the colonies or post colonies (Mignolo, 2005). Mignolo states that globalization is a continuation of modes of socio/economic authority and power that emerged in the construction of capitalism as a modern/ colonial world system. Colonial difference refers to the geopolitics of how knowledge was, and is, produced, accessed and reproduced within that complex historical context. In Mignolo's words, it is:

the difference between centre and periphery, between the Euro-centric critique of Eurocentrism and knowledge production by those who participated in building the modern/colonial world and those who have been left out of the discussion (p. 63).

We think this set of ideas about geo-politics of knowledge production pertains to the themes being pursued in this volume. What the editors refer to as epistemologies from the North and South, are metaphoric reflections of conditions of knowledge production in the post-colonial world where we are located. This volume is highlighting that those who have been left out are now not only participating in the production of knowledge but also in *how* that knowledge is to be attained or collected, that is, *methodology*. For us, it is not a question about what methods are appropriate to fit the context of research in the South, but whether the methods are being composed or performed in order to decolonize the control over knowledge production. This is where the reality of coevalness of ethnographic encounters becomes important.

Forms of collective praxis can emerge from these encounters. Thus, primary school students in Oaxaca can be active participants in what will constitute knowledge for them, Oaxacan university students can claim their own right to representation, and inmates in the state prison of Oaxaca can move into spaces of artistic and aesthetic production. Further, since we as ethnographers are also performing within the same time and space domains, we have the means to collect a diversity of data on these activities that can be presented in an array of narrative fashions that can add to these multilingual/multicultural achievements. In general terms, the history of knowledge production in the North has sought to express itself in a monolingual voice as the logical and empirical authority (Quijano, 2007). Given that ethnographic encounters are performative activities of all the participants, they all have to move within all the linguistic and cultural stages where these performances take place. This calls for skills of critical action and reflexivity. These various multilingual and multicultural performances subvert the claims of the monolingual authority, and suggest that new domains of epistemology and aesthetics are possible (Sommer, 2004).

These are our humble thoughts on the perils, pitfalls and reflexivity of qualitative research in education.

References

Canagarajah, S., 'Changing Communicative Needs, Revised Assessment Objectives: Testing English as an International Language', *Language Assessment Quarterly*, 3 (3) (2006), 229–242.

Castells, M., *The Information Age: Economy, Society, and Culture—The Power of Identity*, Vol. 2 (Oxford: Blackwell Publishers, 2000).

Clemente, A., and Higgins, M., *Performing English with a Post-colonial Accent: Ethnographic Narratives from Mexico* (London: Tufnell Press, 2008).

Clemente, A., and Higgins, M., 'Flying over Prison Walls: The Praxis of Language Performances with a Post-colonial Accent—An Ethnographic Encounter in Oaxaca, Mexico', Paper presented at the Centre for Latin American and Caribbean Studies, Brown University, Providence, Rhode Island (12 April 2009).

Clemente, A., Dantas, M., and Higgins, M., 'Ethnographic Encounters with Young Language Learners in an Urban Primary School of Oaxaca', *MEXTESOL*, 33(1) (2009), 13–30.

Dietz, G., *Multiculturalismo, Interculturalidad y Educacion* (Granada: Universidad de Granada, 2003).

Fabian, J., *Memory against Culture* (Durham: Duke University Press, 2007).

Freire, P., and Donald, M., *Literacy: Reading the Word and the World* (South Hadley, MA: Bergin and Garvey, 1987).

García Canclini, N., *Diferentes, Desiguales y Desconectados: Mapas de La Interculturalidad* (Barcelona: Gedisa Editorial, 2004).

Hernández Díaz, J., (ed.). *Ciudadanías Diferenciadas en un Estado Multicultural: Los Usos y Costumbres en Oaxaca* (Mexico, D.F.: Siglo Veintiuno Editores/ UABJO, 2007).

Kumaravadivelu, B., *Beyond Methods: Macrostrategies for Language Teaching* (New Havens and London: Yale University Press, 2003).

Kumaravadivelu, B., *Understanding Language Teaching: From Method to Post-method* (Mahwah, New Jersey: Lawrence Erlbaum Associates, Inc., 2006).

Kumaravadivelu, B., 'Interrogating Cultural Complexities in the Classroom', Plenary presented at the Second International Qualitative Research Conference, Guanajuato, Guanajuato, Mexico (30 May, 2007).

Larsen-Freeman, D., *Techniques and Principles in Language Teaching*, 2e (Oxford: Oxford University Press, 2000).

Mignolo, W., 'Prophets Facing Sidewise: The Geopolitics of Knowledge and the Colonial Difference', *Social Epistemology*, 19 (1) (2005), 111–127.

Moll, L., Amanti, C., Neff, D., and Gonzalez, N., 'Funds of Knowledge for Teaching: Using a Qualitative Approach to Connect Homes and Classrooms', *Theory into Practice*, I (2), Qualitative Issues in Educational Research (1992), 132–141.

Purcell-Gates, V., (ed.), *Cultural Practices of Literacy: Case Studies of Language, Literacy, Social Practices, and Power* (London: L. Erlbaum Associates, Publishers, 2007).

Quijano, A., 'Coloniality and Modernity/Rationality', *Cultural Studies*, 21 (2–3) (March/May 2007), 449–514.

Street, B., *Social Literacies: Critical Approaches to Literacy in Development, Ethnography and Education* (London: Longman, 1995).

Sommer, D., *Bilingual Aesthetics: A New Sentimental Education* (Durham: Duke University Press, 2004).

Velez-Ibanez, C., and Greenberg, J., 'Formation and Transformation of Funds of Knowledge among U.S.–Mexican Households', in *Anthropology and Education Quarterly*, 23 (4) (1992), 313–335.

Appendix: The two versions of a poem

VALOR

Enardecido en el hombre el cual
nunca se demuestra lo contrario por
ser motivo de vergüenza, simbolo de
orgullo para el ser humano al sentir algo
amargo en el gusto de no demostrarlo, rojiza
sensación, con un fuerte zumbido de grandeza
como algo agradable al olfato al percibirlo

Valor

Enardecido en el hombre,
Es símbolo de orgullo.
Es rojiza sensación,
Es fuerte zumbido de grandeza,
Es un aroma agradable al olfato.

No demostrar el valor,
Es motivo de vergüenza,
Es un sabor amargo en el gusto.

Editors

Dr Fauzia Shamim is Professor of Applied Linguistics and Chairperson of the Department of English, University of Karachi, Karachi, Pakistan. Till recently, she was working as a full-time teacher educator and researcher at the Aga Khan University, Institute for Educational Development (AKU-IED), Karachi, Pakistan. Dr Shamim has extensive experience of conducting qualitative research and supervising research students from different countries in Central and South Asia and Eastern Africa, studying in Pakistan. She has written several research reports and published research papers in books and journals. She has also presented research papers at both national and international conferences.

As a founder member of the recently formed Research Special Interest Group of the Society of Pakistan English Language Teachers, the Pakistan Association for Research in Education (PARE), and the Qualitative Research Interest Group (QRIG) at the Aga Khan University, Karachi, Dr Shamim is working actively for the promotion of qualitative research methods in education in Pakistan and other countries in the South. Dr Shamim has served as Chair of the Research and Policy Studies Advisory Committee at AKU-IED. She was also a member of the Aga Khan University's Ethical Review Committee. Email address: fauzia.shamim@yahoo.com

Dr Rashida Qureshi is Director, Arts and Sciences, at the National Institute of Health and Social Sciences, Islamabad. Till recently, she was Assistant Professor at the Aga Khan University, Institute for Educational Development, (AKU-IED), Karachi, Pakistan. She has been involved in preparing teacher-educators through teaching in the Masters and PhD in Education programmes. Prior to joining AKU-IED in 2003, she was working as community development practitioner. She has extensive experience of working directly with rural women in the remotest regions of the North West Frontier Province of Pakistan (now called Khyber Pakhtoonkhwa). She has written several research reports. She has also published articles in international journals. Dr Qureshi was also a member of the Aga Khan University's Ethics Review Committee. Her recent publications include *Gender in Education in Pakistan* with Jane Rareiya (OUP, 2007) and *Schools and Schooling Practices: Lessons for Policy and Practice* with Fauzia Shamim (OUP, 2009). Email address: rashidaqureshi_sm@yahoo.com

Contributors

Dilshad Ashraf is Assistant Professor and Head of Research and Policy Studies at the Aga Khan University's Institute for Educational Development (AKU-IED). Curriculum studies, gender in education, and school improvement are the main focus of her research and teaching at the institute.

Saiqa Imtiaz Asif is Professor and Director, English Language Centre, Bahauddin Zakariya University Multan. She has a Ph.D. from Lancaster University, and M.Sc. from the University of Edinburgh. Her areas of interest include ELT, Sociolinguistics and Research Methodology. She has published a number of research papers related to these fields. She has participated in international conferences held in the USA, UK, Japan, Egypt and Pakistan. Currently, she is doing research in sociolinguistics with particular reference to the Pakistani languages.

Ángeles Clemente has been working for more than twenty years at the *Facultad de Idiomas* at the *Universidad Autónoma "Benito Juárez" de Oaxaca* in the city of Oaxaca, Mexico. Her areas of research and teaching are in Applied Linguistics and Second Language Acquisition. Her research focus has moved from a socio-cognitive approach in learning towards a socio-cultural focus on activities of learning English as an additional language. This shift in her research interests can be noted in her current book (co-authored by M. Higgins) *Performing English with a Post-Colonial Accent: Ethnographic Narratives from Mexico* (2008). Email address: angelesclemente@gmail.com

Michael James Higgins is an anthropologist from the United States who has been doing urban ethnographic research in the city of Oaxaca for more than 40 years. He is a Professor Emeritus of Anthropology from the University of Northern Colorado in Greeley, Colorado. His research has been focused on issues of gender, sexuality, ethnicity, and social class dynamics among the urban poor and working class of the city of Oaxaca. Currently, he has been doing collaborative ethnographic research with A. Clemente on language, culture, and identity in Oaxaca. He is the co-author with Clemente on the book *Performing English with Post-Colonial Accent: Ethnographic Narratives from Mexico* (2008). He is an affiliated member of the Cuerpo Academico en Linguistica Aplicada Critica de la *Facultad de Idiomas* at the *Universidad Autónoma "Benito Juárez" de Oaxaca*. Email address: mjhiggi55@hotmail.com.

Adrian Holliday is Professor of Applied Linguistics at Canterbury Christ Church University where he supervises doctoral research in social and cultural issues related to English in international settings. He is also Head of The

Graduate School and manages the university-wide Ph.D. programme and its relationship with the university research culture. He is author of *The Struggle to Teach English as an International Language*, (OUP, 2005), *Intercultural Communication*, (Routledge, 2004) (with Hyde and Kullman), and *Doing and Writing Qualitative Research* (Sage, 2nd edition, 2007). He was an English teacher in Iran in the 1970s and a university curriculum consultant in Syria and Egypt in the 1980s. His current research interests include chauvinistic cultural imaginations of the non-Western Other in everyday life, and alternative methods of data collection and analysis in qualitative research.

Mehri Honarbin-Holliday is an Iranian born academic who lives and works in England. She is a Senior Research Fellow in international education at Canterbury Christ Church University, and affiliated to the London Middle East Institute. She is also a practicing artist and works interdisciplinary exploring the intersections of gender, identity, and art. She is the author of 'Becoming Visible in Iran: Women in Contemporary Iranian Society' (2008), where the voices of young women in Iran and their activisms are projected alongside their sense of autonomy and agency. Women's narratives in 'Becoming visible in Iran' are far from the stereotyped misperceptions about Muslim women in the West. Visual culture is integral to Mehri's work; she has exhibited her video and fired clay installations in Iran, Britain, Mexico, and the United States and is the recipient of the 2007 national award from the Art and Culture Secretariat at Tehran Municiality. Her current research projects include an ESREA EU-wide inter-university project at Canterbury Christ Church University, and forms in masculinities and patriarchy in Iran for a new book.

Almina Pardhan was a middle school and high school teacher for several years in Canada before becoming a teacher educator in the area of early childhood education and gender at the Aga Khan University-Institute for Educational Development in Karachi, Pakistan. Her areas of interest are early childhood education, gender, and research processes. She has been involved in research projects on women's experiences of school, work, and health in Pakistan. She has also conducted research on children's gender experiences of play in Pakistan. She has recently completed her doctorate degree in Early Childhood Education and Gender from the Ontario Institute for Studies in Education, University of Toronto.

Jane Rareiya was a high school teacher for several years before she became a teacher educator and worked with teachers in the East African Region and Pakistan. She has also been involved in school improvement projects in Tanzania and Kenya. Jane is presently teaching at the Aga Khan University, Institute for Educational Development, Eastern Africa located in Dar es Salaam, Tanzania. Her areas of interest are reflective practice, gender and educational leadership. She has recently completed her doctorate degree in Gender and Educational Management from the University of Keele, Staffordshire, UK.